Table of Contents

Prologue

Part Three – Understanding Utopia

Chapter 8 – Imagine

Chapter 9 – Cogitator

Chapter 10 – Utopian Handbook

Prologue

When serving in Vietnam (in the Navy,) I became the captain's phone talker and saw all the action from the bridge. The ship's communication system is vital. Talkers are issued voice-activated phones that plug into a special outlet and strap behind the neck with earphones attached. The mouthpiece has a button that, when depressed, allows the voice vibrations to generate enough current to broadcast messages to all other phones plugged into the system. All of them are active at all stations during combat and refueling. For all docking, departures, refueling and battle conditions, I relayed orders from the bridge to all stations in the ship.

My first combat experience on the bridge with the captain was memorable:

General Quarters sounded and I reported to the bridge with my phone and plugged in. We were steaming toward shore with two other ships, the USS Stoddard, another destroyer and the USS Canberra, a cruiser. Destroyers have four cannon mounts - 51, 52, (forward) 53, and 54 (aft) from prow to stern. The gun barrels are five inches across and the bullet can go five miles. That's why the number five precedes their position. Cruisers can fire eight miles. The Stoddard and we were to soften up an area near the beach to enable Marine helicopters to swoop in and drop their men to take the position. The Canberra would be firing deeper up the hills to destroy gun emplacements. We reached our positions and opened fire. Explosions of quick succession on the beach were on their mark by both ships.

As I watched the action, I became a live reporter for the rest of the ship, something that had not been done before. I would be thanked by the crew many times for this. It is not easy to be in the belly of a ship in combat without any knowledge of the goings-on topside, so I was just a roving reporter for my mates. They truly appreciated the relief from not knowing.

Suddenly, I saw flashes on the beach and reacted:

"Captain, shore batteries, shore batteries!" I roared.

The captain turned to the helmsman. In a loud voice:

"Quartermaster, what's our attitude?"

"275 North, sir!" came the reply.

"Come to starboard 10 degrees. All engines full!" the captain bellows.

The explosions were all around our ship, both from cannons and rockets. Several were close, but we had already begun evasive maneuvers. (Artillerymen use "patterns" to target an objective and zero in on the exact range to adjust their guns accordingly.) A moving target three miles away is not so easy to pattern. That's the reason for fast evasive reaction.

Ten seconds later:

"Come to port ten degrees, full speed ahead!" We zigzagged back and forth every few seconds until we weaved our way out of range. The Stoddard was hit and lost a couple of men. The Canberra was winged, but not seriously.

When General Quarters was called off, I returned to the office and pondered the captain's words. I had never heard the word "attitude" used in the context of the captain's orders. It then dawned on me that, if we don't like what we see in front of us, we can always change our attitude. That life lesson instilled itself in me permanently that day.

Another significant event happened when we stopped in Guam for refueling. We were to spend the day there and split the crew into two groups to go ashore for a break. I went in the morning to do some sightseeing and gawk at the goony birds. They are one funny avian to behold. No fear, slow-motion waddle, hilarious. Returning to the ship's office for some reading, I suddenly hear the General Quarters alarm and grab my phone to head for the bridge. I got there just before the captain and immediately noticed his florid face. He was obviously drunk. Not good.

A Russian trawler was offshore a few miles from our ship. Their only purpose at the time was surveillance and intelligence gathering. The captain issued orders to head for it. When we got there, he ordered all garbage to be taken to the fantail and made the helmsman circle the trawler at what appeared to be a too close distance. We dumped garbage all around the trawler to attempt to foul up their surveillance readings. After the garbage was depleted, he seemed to get angrier and barked:

"S..., tell the crew to prepare to ram!"

I did no such thing. I faced him and said:

"Captain, we only have half the crew on board. If something goes wrong, there may be some repercussions."

His face went from red to white. He gave orders to return to shore.

After a stop in Hawaii for a pleasant three days, we finally docked in our home port - San Diego. Not long after, a change of command procedure took place for our next deployment. This is a very ceremonial event where the entire crew forms a phalanx on board for the exiting captain and to welcome the new captain. There usually is strict adherence to protocol in the process. However, a slight change occurred as the Captain was walking past me; he stopped and looked at me and said:

"Thanks, S...."

We have a drunken captain commanding our ship of state and we need to change our attitude to get back on the correct course. His orders are endangering the crew.

Why we need each other

As the world began to ring in 2018, UN Secretary-General Antonio Guterres called for global unity to overcome growing challenges.

In his New Year message on Sunday, New Years' Eve, Guterres said the world appeared to have "gone in reverse" before adding, "On New Year's Day 2018 I am not issuing an appeal, I am issuing an alert -- a red alert for our world."

He continued: "As we begin 2018, I call for unity. ... We can settle conflicts, overcome hatred and defend shared values. But we can only do that together."

Reflecting on his January message when he assumed the secretary-general position -- in which he called for peace -- Guterres said that conflicts have deepened, global anxieties about nuclear weapons have increased, inequalities have grown and nationalism and xenophobia are on the rise.

He stressed cooperation and collaboration should be the way forward in 2018, saying: "Unity is the path. Our future depends on it."

He then urged leaders "everywhere to make this New Year's resolution: Narrow the gaps. Bridge the divides. Rebuild trust by bringing people together around common goals."

Global Warming (and/or Warning)

Even if greenhouse emissions stopped overnight the concentrations already in the atmosphere would still mean a global rise of between 0.5 and 1C. A shift of a single degree is barely perceptible to human skin, but it's not human skin we're talking about - it's the planet; and an average increase of one degree across its entire surface means huge changes in climatic extremes.

Six thousand years ago, when the world was one degree warmer than it is now, the American agricultural heartland around Nebraska was desert. It suffered a short reprise during the dust- bowl years of the 1930s, when the topsoil blew away and hundreds of thousands of refugees trailed through the dust to an uncertain welcome further west. The effect of one-degree warming, therefore, requires no great feat of imagination.

While tropical lands teeter on the brink, the Arctic already may have passed the point of no return. Warming near the pole is much faster than the global average, with the result that Arctic icecaps and glaciers have lost 400 cubic kilometers of ice in 40 years. Permafrost - ground that has lain frozen for thousands of years, is dissolving into mud and lakes, destabilizing whole areas as the ground collapses beneath buildings, roads and pipelines. As polar bears and Inuit are being pushed off the top of the planet, previous predictions are starting to look optimistic. Earlier snowmelt means more summer heat goes into the air and ground rather than into melting snow, raising temperatures in a positive feedback effect. More dark shrubs and forest on formerly bleak tundra means still more heat is absorbed by vegetation.

Chance of avoiding one degree of global warming: zero.

BETWEEN ONE AND TWO DEGREES OF WARMING

At this level, expected within 40 years, the hot European summer of 2003 will be the annual norm. Anything that could be called a heat wave thereafter will be of Saharan intensity. Even in average years, many people will die of heat stress.

Once body temperature reaches 41C (104F) its thermoregulatory system begins to break down. Sweating ceases and breathing becomes shallow and rapid. The pulse quickens, and the victim may lapse into a coma. Unless drastic measures are taken to reduce the body's core temperature, the brain is starved of oxygen and vital organs begin to fail. Death will be only minutes away unless the emergency services can quickly get the victim into intensive care.

BETWEEN TWO AND THREE DEGREES OF WARMING

Up to this point, assuming that governments have planned carefully and farmers have converted to more appropriate crops, not too many people outside subtropical Africa need have starved. Beyond two degrees, however, preventing mass starvation will be as easy as halting the cycles of the moon. First millions, then billions, of people will face an increasingly tough battle to survive.

The end of humanity (along with most organic life) is nigh. A three-degree increase in global temperature - possible as early as 2050 - would throw the carbon cycle into reverse. Instead of absorbing carbon dioxide, vegetation and soils start to release it. So much carbon pours into the atmosphere that it pumps up atmospheric concentrations by 250 parts per million by 2100, boosting global warming by another 1.5C. In other words, the Hadley team had discovered that carbon-cycle feedbacks could tip the planet into runaway global warming by the middle of this century - much earlier than anyone had expected.

In the US and Australia, people will curse the climate-denying governments of Trump and Howard. No matter what later administrations may do, it will not be enough to keep the mercury down. With new "super-hurricanes" growing from the warming sea, Houston could be destroyed by 2045, and Australia will be a death trap. Farming and food production will tip into irreversible decline. Salt water will creep up the stricken rivers, poisoning ground water. Higher temperatures mean greater evaporation, further drying out vegetation and soils, and causing huge losses from reservoirs. In state capitals, heat every year is likely to kill between 8,000 and 15,000 mainly elderly people.

BETWEEN THREE AND FOUR DEGREES OF WARMING

The stream of refugees will now include those fleeing from coasts to safer interiors - millions at a time when storms hit. Where they persist, coastal cities will become fortified islands. The world economy, too, will be threadbare. As direct losses, social instability and insurance payouts cascade through the system, the funds to support displaced people will be increasingly scarce. Sea levels will be rampaging upwards - in this temperature range, both poles are certain to melt, causing an eventual rise of 50 meters. "I am not suggesting it would be instantaneous. In fact it would take centuries, and probably millennia, to melt all of the Antarctic's ice. But it could yield sea-level rises of a meter or so every 20 years - far beyond our capacity to adapt. Oxford would sit on one of many coastlines in a UK reduced to an archipelago of tiny islands.

BETWEEN FOUR AND FIVE DEGREES OF WARMING

We are looking now at an entirely different planet. Ice sheets have vanished from both poles; rainforests have burnt up and turned to desert; the dry and lifeless Alps resemble the High Atlas; rising seas are scouring deep into continental interiors. One temptation may be to shift populations from dry areas to the newly thawed regions of the far north, in Canada and Siberia. Even here, though, summers may be too hot for crops to be grown away from the coasts; and there is no guarantee that northern governments will admit southern refugees. Lynas recalls James Lovelock's suspicion that Siberia and Canada would be invaded by China and the US, each hammering another nail into humanity's coffin. Any armed conflict, particularly involving nuclear weapons, would of course further increase the planetary surface area uninhabitable for humans.

If people continue to resist truth for the purpose of money, future generations will disappear. Whether or not Mother Earth will recover from the folly of humans is yet to be determined. Even if humanity is but a small contributor to a natural change, there is no logical reason to devastate our environment. The race for sanity is up to each and every one of us. Get involved for the sake of your children and grandchildren.

"Trumping the System" has little to do with the egomaniacal bully in Washington, although some of his idiocies are worth mentioning. It is about examining the current governmental system and its components with the intent of improving life on earth for all its inhabitants. It is fact that systems have to either be changed from inside or entirely replaced by a new one. A total replacement would cause mass hysteria, beating of breasts and a probable stampede towards suicide. Uniting our minds to introduce a process that can make a calmer transition is wise.

It is important to realize that each one of us holds a trump in this card game. Anyone who plays card games is aware that a trump suit stops the opponents' control and ends their domination. Our trump card is our individual power. We can give it away or create a different base of power.

"Everything we do, everything we are, rests on our personal power. If we have enough of it, one word is enough to change the course of our lives. If we don't have enough, the most magnificent piece of wisdom can be revealed to us and that revelation won't make a damn bit of difference. Do you know that at this very moment you are surrounded by eternity? And do you know you can use that eternity, if you so desire? Do you know that you can extend our self forever in any direction and use it to take the totality of our self forever in any direction? Do you know that one moment can be eternity? If you had enough personal power, my words alone would serve as a means to round up the totality of your self and get to the crucial part of it out of the boundaries in which it is contained."
Carlos Castaneda from "Tales of Power"

Systems analysis and design requires understanding of a number of concepts. The first one is that all systems must be connected to every other system in order to survive. That means that all subsidiary activities within a system should support the system objective(s). Identifying those that do not and removing or altering them to comply will automatically make the overall system operate better. A well-designed system has:

Organization: Organization implies structure and order. It is the *arrangement* of components that helps to achieve the objectives.

Interaction: refers to the manner in which each component functions with other component of the system.

Interdependence: means that parts of the organization depend on one another. One subsystem depends upon the input of another subsystem for proper functioning and output of one subsystem is the required input for another subsystem.

Integration: is concerned with how a system is tied together. This means that parts of the system work together within the system even though each part performs a unique function - like a project team integrates.

Central Objective: The last characteristic of a system is its central objective. All activities should aim at the same target. It is critical that an accurate understanding of the Big Picture be shared by the participants.

The base unit of society is the individual. It is this system that must be understood first.

Utopian Dreams

"Imagination is more important than knowledge." Albert Einstein.

"The problems of the world cannot possibly be solved by skeptics and cynics whose horizons are limited by obvious realities. We need men and women who can dream of things that never were." John F. Kennedy

"How long shall man wander in darkness, looking for wisdom when it is in himself - and he does not know it? It is the higher principle of our nature. Now let this higher principle rise with me above all the opinions of men about another world and come up hither and sit on the clouds made by superstition and look and survey one vast space where perfect light and harmony exist. Now turn your eyes to the earth and see men's eyes turned upward to see this world and listen to their stories about it. See them down on their knees begging an unknown God to guide them to this world. So the superstition in regard to it is that the spirits of all those that they have created and believed in come from this vast place where men never come nor ever will come till he breaks the fetters of idolatry and by the buoyancy of his wisdom rises by his own wisdom unfettered by superstitions into the glorious light of science." Dr. Phineas P. Quimby, Founder of New Thought and healer of Mary Baker-Eddy (mid-19th Century)

We are creators existing in Creation. Whatever we imagine can be created. That is actually how we go through our waking day. We imagine taking a shower-BAM! - we're clean. We imagine going to work-BAM! - we're there. We imagine having a family, not so BAM. It takes a lot of thought and planning to have the wedding of our choice and the following events. But yet, it is the imagination that lets us make those plans and make them occur. How we prioritize those imaginations in our mind at this time, in this place, under these circumstances determines what action we will take next. We are always communicating with ourselves, thinking of what to do next.

Every action we take is to achieve some goal. That goal must first be imagined before we can bring it to fruition. Whether it is to take our morning shower, go on a vacation, walk the dog or any number of other objectives, we must first envision them with imagination. To reach the objective of living in Utopia, it is the result we must describe first, not the actions we take to get it. There is a myriad of methods to achieve any goal.

Goal achievement is a three-part system that resembles a recipe. All systems have the same three components – Input, Process and Output and all systems have to be connected to every other system in order to be valid. Just like creating a delicious meal, we have to imagine the finished product (output), gather the ingredients (input) and put them through a sequential process. So it is with cooking up the ideal of Utopian Life.

Goals are actually prioritized as their value MINUS the effort required to achieve them. Every life form is busy in every moment activating itself on its number one priority as dictated by the individual's value system. There are no exceptions to this rule. Everyone reading these words is spending time on their number one priority at this time, at this place, under these circumstances. If your tea kettle calls you or your smoke alarm goes off, you will be distracted and address your new number one priority. Most people seldom address their goal valuations but it will eventually be essential to do so in order to create a sane and safe Utopia. If the prologue is not enough to make the reader prioritize daily goals differently, there is no sense in continuing reading.

What would the goal to create a Utopian society mean to humanity?

Utopia is a kind and gentle place. There are no homeless people in it. It is an egalitarian society where no individual is ignored. There are many examples of imagined Utopias in history from Plato, Thomas More and others. The Hippie movement in the 1960s created a number of communes intended to provide solace to the weary by ridding themselves of the corporate world and decadent objectives. There is one major difference between those ideals and the one we are able to create today - Technology. In Utopia, technology is the slave of humanity, rather than the other way around as it is today. To achieve that reversal, the existing ruling class must move aside.

What prevents us from creating the ideal of Utopia?

Everything humans believe and value is based upon agreements among themselves. They form groups that communicate and bolster beliefs and values they desire to hold as true, or real, and live their life according to the mandates of the group(s) to which they want to belong. This is the basic herding instinct of social animals - which we are. Birds of a feather group together. In Utopia, there is only one group and it is all-inclusive.

Splinter groups are created by "Group-Think," or Collective Consciousness of their members. When a laboratory technician wants to see the development of a culture, he places a "seed" in a petri dish containing agar and watches the development. This is similar to placing an idea in society and watching how it affects the population as it becomes an ism. Cultures separate themselves by agreeing to trains of thought that may differentiate them from other groups. Their behavior is governed by the indoctrination of dogma into their group-think. This dogma is also called a tenet – (French for "to hold,") or ism. Today's society has too many isms that create separation instead of unification, like racism, sexism, Fascism, etc.

Indoctrination: The process of teaching a person or group to accept a set of beliefs uncritically.

"The United States is unusual among the industrial democracies in the rigidity of the system of ideological control - 'indoctrination', we might say - exercised through the mass media." Noam Chomsky

Mass media indoctrinate people and groups through constant bombardment of confusing messages. They spout isms to program underdeveloped minds into doing things that serve the masters. In the UK, television programming that uses flash ads (microseconds of message to influence the subconscious) have to place a warning at the beginning of the show. How could that do any good if the show gets watched anyway? Does this not indicate that mind control is prevalent in the media?

The purpose for flash ads and subliminal advertising is to inject a thought into our subconscious. If you are familiar with the phrase "My life flashed before my eyes," stated by someone that had a near-death experience, you can realize that our subconscious is akin to a life recorder. There is no experience that is forgotten by this ability. Nikola Tesla's could recite a book verbatim immediately after he read it. This suggests he was able to access this power.

Once a thought is injected into the subconscious, it can be activated by a "trigger" in the future. This is mind control at its finest.

Communicating ideas and ideals is not easy. Accuracy of the messages being exchanged necessitates agreeing on the meaning of the programs being downloaded into the brain as well as how they influence our decisions.

"Wisdom begins with the definition of terms." Socrates

Imperialism: A policy of extending a country's power and influence through colonization, use of military force, or other means. "The sun never sets on the British Empire" is a saying that may still ring true and exemplifies imperialism. Millions of Native Americans murdered and disenfranchised for the sake of extending power and influence is imperialism. Starting wars in the Middle East and elsewhere is imperialism.

"The truth is that neither British nor American imperialism was or is idealistic. It has always been driven by economic or strategic interests." Charley Reese

Fascism: An authoritarian and nationalistic right-wing system of government and social organization. If we watch the North Korean army marching in locked, goose-stepping order, we can visualize what Fascism may resemble. Hitler's Gestapo has morphed into a militarized police force in most capitalistic countries.

"They claim to be super patriots, but they would destroy every liberty guaranteed by the Constitution. They demand free enterprise, but are the spokesmen for monopoly and vested interest. Their final objective toward all their deceit is directed is to capture political power so that, using the power of the state and the power of the market simultaneously, they may keep the common man in eternal subjection." Vice President Henry Wallace (speaking of American Fascists)

"Fascism is capitalism in decay." Vladimir Lenin

Racism: Prejudice, discrimination, or antagonism directed against someone of a different race based on the belief that one's own race is superior. Not much more need be said after watching the news. It is not caused by hate, but rather by fear. The only thing that causes fear is ignorance.

"Racism is man's gravest threat to man - the maximum of hatred for a minimum of reason." Abraham Joshua Heschel

Sexism: Prejudice, stereotyping, or discrimination, typically against women, on the basis of sex. Again, the current news broadcasts surely make us more aware of this ism. It is one of the corrupt behaviors of a patriarchal and egotistical society.

"I mean, what is racism? Racism is a projection of our own fears onto another person. What is sexism? It's our own vulnerability about our potency and masculinity projected as our need to subjugate another person, you know? Fascism, the same thing: People are trying to untidy our state, so I legislate as a way of controlling my environment." Gary Ross

Patriotism: The quality of being patriotic; devotion to and vigorous support for one's country. Any government who thinks exclusion from the rest of the world is a good idea needs to be analyzed for insanity. This is a good example of selfish conservatism, again caused by fear.

"Heroism on command, senseless violence, and all the loathsome nonsense that goes by the name of patriotism - how passionately I hate them!" Albert Einstein

"Guard against the impostures of pretended patriotism." George Washington

Egotism: The fact of being excessively conceited or absorbed in oneself. This is caused by taking undue credit for being what we are. Ego is the only element in the universe that tries to separate itself from it. Its worst attribute is judging. It is patriotism in an individual.

"Egotism is the anesthetic that dulls the pain of stupidity." Frank Leahy

Conservatism: Commitment to traditional values and ideas with opposition to change or innovation.

The conservative mind is incapable of innovation and creativity. It only knows how to use people and resources for its own goals. Creating wage slaves and mind control are the methods used. If conservatives at the turn of the nineteenth century had any vision, our airlines would be named Union Pacific, Santa Fe, Burlington Northern, etc. Conservatives couldn't even see the connection of commercial transportation to any other method than rail. They maintain control by keeping the truth from their workers and threatening dissenters.

"Republicans today have given the country conservatism in the spirit of Sarah Palin, whose ignorance about the world, contempt for expertise, and raw appeals to white identity politics presaged Trump's incendiary campaign." George Packer

Liberalism: a political philosophy based on belief in progress, the essential goodness of the human race, and the autonomy of the individual and standing for the protection of political and civil liberties; specifically: such a philosophy that considers government as a crucial instrument for amelioration of social inequities (such as those involving race, gender, or class).

"...someone who looks ahead and not behind, someone who welcomes new ideas without rigid reactions, someone who cares about the welfare of the people – their health, their housing, their schools, their jobs, their civil rights, and their civil liberties – someone who believes we can break through the stalemate and suspicions that grip us in our policies abroad. If that is was they mean by a Liberal, then I'm proud to say: 'I'm a Liberal.'" John F. Kennedy

"I suffer from the same frustration that every decent American suffers from. That is, that you begin to wonder whether decent liberal instincts, decent humanitarian instincts, can actually penetrate the right-wing voice, get through the steering of American opinion by the mass media." John le Carre

Socialism: A political and economic theory of social organization which advocates that the means of production, distribution, and exchange should be owned or regulated by the community as a whole.

"Democratic socialism means that we must reform a political system that is corrupt, that we must create an economy that works for all, not just the very wealthy." Bernie Sanders

Anarchism: Belief in the abolition of all government and the organization of society on a voluntary, cooperative basis without recourse to force or compulsion. Self-control and self-governance are both necessary to be an anarchist. Anarchy does not mean chaos or disorder; it means freedom from an oppressive centralized authority with a monopoly on force.

"Anarchism means all sort of things to different people, but the traditional anarchists' movements assumed that

there'd be a highly organized society, just one organized from below with direct participation and so on." Noam Chomsky

Communism: A theory or system of social organization in which all property is owned by the community and each person contributes and receives according to their ability and needs. This can work only if money is eliminated. It is the natural order of things. Once people start amassing money to gain power over others, they become slave masters.

"The theory of Communism may be summed up in one sentence: Abolish all private property." Karl Marx

Humanism: A rationalist outlook or system of thought attaching prime importance to human rather than divine or supernatural matters.

"For humanism also appeals to man as man. It seeks to liberate the universal qualities of human nature from the narrow limitations of blood and soil and class and to create a common language and a common culture in which men can realize their common humanity." Christopher Dawson

Humanitarianism: The promotion of human welfare.

"Humanitarianism consists in never sacrificing a human being to a purpose." Albert Schweitzer

Capitalism: An economic and political system in which a country's trade and industry are controlled by private owners for profit, rather than by the state. All businesses and corporations should be owned by the employees to make capitalism desirable.

"Capitalism is against the things that we say we believe in - democracy, freedom of choice, fairness. It's not about any of those things now. It's about protecting the wealthy and legalizing greed." Michael Moore

"America is just the country that how all the written guarantees in the world for freedom are no protection against tyranny and oppression of the worst kind. There the politician has come to be looked upon as the very scum of society." Peter Kropotkin

Narcissism: The pursuit of gratification from vanity or egotistic admiration of one's own attributes. The term originated from the Greek mythology, where the young Narcissus fell in love with his own image reflected in a pool of water. It is the glorification of the body as opposed to spiritual pursuit.

"Narcissism falls along the axis of what psychologists call personality disorders, one of a group that includes antisocial, dependent, histrionic, avoidant and borderline personalities. But by most measures, narcissism is one of the worst, if only because the narcissists themselves are so clueless." Jeffrey Kluger

An ism in a computer is a program, application (APP) or system. When downloading an APP into a smartphone, we inject it with a train of thought intended to perform a specific function or process when we touch the icon (trigger) for that application. Indoctrinated isms activate humans that same way. We can actually send the undesirable isms we downloaded into our brains to the trash bin. We have to open our minds to this realization in order to change.

Closed minds are either useless or dangerous. Open-mindedness is one of the least valued and least developed, yet most desperately needed mental skills if we are to navigate our way to a thriving world. The sense of wonder we were given at birth dissipates too quickly in the face of "authority." Most of what we learned about history, economics, politics, ethics and even science turns out not to be true. Assumptions are pieces of knowledge that do not belong in the Big Picture of Utopia. We can't trust government, bankers or media, yet they dominate the communication of our information. We simply have to think critically and for ourselves, and that has to start with opening our thinking to consider new ideas and information.

Each individual aspiring for understanding and growth has to reflect upon the isms that affect their decisions. Isms are just "trains of thought" or "schools of thought" inflicted on us by others and those trains sometimes take us to places we don't want to be.

Self-Understanding and Self-Control

"Self-examination is the key to insight, which is the key to wisdom." M. Scott Peck

"Without self-knowledge, without understanding the working and functions of his machine, man cannot be free, he cannot govern himself and he will always remain a slave." - G. I. Gurdjieff

Thinking of creating Utopia means we have to take responsibility for our view and think beyond the isms we have adopted. We must think "outside the box."

Zig Ziglar was a good old boy from Texas and a motivational speaker. He was a big part of the self-help movement along with Napoleon Hill, Og Mandino, W. Clement Stone, Norman Vincent Peale and others. He has a wonderful way of blending his talks with homey anecdotes that make sense. One of these anecdotes is about a flea circus. He starts speaking:

"In the old days, when entertainment was hard to come by, traveling circuses would wend their way from town to town across the West and set up camp just outside each burg. They would form a midway of tents for the folks to

amble past. Oddities and performers would be contained in the tents and the populace would pay some charge to enter. Usually, one of these had a flea circus.

The barker outside would entice the folks to enter and, when the tent was full, he would retreat into it and close the entry. Inside were a table covered with a white tablecloth and a large jar atop it covered by another white cloth. The man would uncover the jar, say a few words, uncap the jar and dump a bunch of fleas onto the tablecloth. The fleas would begin jumping up and down, but would not leave the tabletop. Applause and egress."

Zig would continue by describing how a flea trainer would achieve this feat. The trainer would catch a bunch of fleas and place them in the jar and watch and wait. Initially, the little beasties would jump as hard as they could to get away, but they would bump against the top and sides of the jar. After a while, they realized how far they could jump without hurting themselves, so they limited their jumps to stop just short of hitting the jar. Voila - a flea circus! Zig ends his anecdote by asking the group: "What would you rather be, a flea or a flea trainer?"

"Men are prisoners of their own mind." Franklin D. Roosevelt

"Everyone is born a genius, but the process of living de-geniuses them." Richard Buckminster Fuller

The majority of the world population is made up of flea mentalities. Their box is any ism they choose to download and is like the training jar - it represents their comfort zone. When some major calamity happens in a community however, many will climb out to give aid and comfort to others. That is the spirit and attitude that needs to be awakened. "Comfort Zone" should include the entire planet and all its inhabitants. Thinking outside the box should include smashing the jar rather than crawling back into it because it also represents a closed mind. To understand what is outside the box, we must have an open mind and first understand the only way to change a system is to change it from within.

Communication is "the sending or receiving of a message that MEANS THE SAME to both sender and receiver." We can be sure that Zig's anecdotal message will mean different things to different readers. For example, if we use the term "iceberg," most flea mentalities would visualize a mass of ice floating on the ocean. Aristotle would point out that, until we consider the iceberg to be mostly beneath the ocean's surface, we would not know what an iceberg truly is. The same analogy applies to human languages. Few people will take the time to truly understand the underlying semantics beneath the surface of their words. (Semantics is the science of meaning and linguistics is the method humans use to convey meaning to one another.) Comparing small talk to deep conversation is similar to comparing ice cubes to icebergs.

To transcend the flea jar from the inside, we must first understand and agree that we actually are limited by our thinking capability, our communication capability and our ability to understand what meaning(s) is/are true. Everyone reading these words will attach different values to the meaning being conveyed, even though the intent is to agree on what "means the same." The term implies that something is doing the thinking and that the box contains the sum total of our thoughts. If thinking outside the box is important enough to the reader, they will seek out new thoughts to improve, increase and understand why they think what they think. This takes time, effort and desire. Most flea mentalities will succumb to whatever they think is "more important" than self-growth before addressing freedom of thought.

All flea jars differ in size and content and change based on topic and situation. An autistic flea may have a huge mathematical jar and a tiny societal jar, for example. A generalist may have a myriad of small jars while specialists develop specific few jars to huge dimensions. All jars in all situations define their size and content by the bundle of thoughts they contain. The thoughts must all be connected to make sense to the flea. When Leonardo da Vinci said:

"Learn to see, everything is connected," he was referring to thoughts. Universal thinking is what will dissolve all jars.

A thought is not a thing; it is a process cycle. The first step in the cycle is Awareness, which could easily mean "Awakeness." Fleas that are content in their jars' comfort zone are sleeping. They have not yet seen, nor attempted to see, the beauty of the universe. Like the Eloi in "The Time Machine," they stay blissfully content to be domesticated pets to be eaten by the Morlocks until the protagonist wakes them up. We can all wake up by paying Attention - the second step of the thought cycle.

Paying attention means to focus one's thought energy to develop the full meaning of the iceberg. This is achieved by seeking the connectivity of any thought to any other thought. A wise person will seek connective thoughts to add to the meaning while the foolish flea will look for differences to justify ending the thought process. The amount of attention one pays to any thought is based upon how interesting it is to the thinker. Patience is in short supply for most fleas, especially in today's societal bedlam of constant technological cacophony.

When we pay attention, it is with the intent of analyzing the value of our thoughts. This value is reached by comparing the meaning of the thought to the overall meaning of our life. It is the value that prioritizes our actions. (In Buddhist philosophy, it is stated that humans can hold a maximum of 87 thoughts in their collection of jars.) Based upon the result of the analysis step value, we will either seek more connections to build the meaning, interrupt the process, or take action. The level of interest will contribute to the decision.

Action in our anecdote is taken because some sense of imbalance is felt by the flea. At first, their imbalance was caused by being confined, so their actions reflected this. When the fleas hit the sides and top of Ziglar's jar, they made an adjustment to their actions to avoid pain. Even when the jar was removed, the fear of pain prevented them from regaining their freedom -- much like many humans.

The last step in the cycle is Adaptation/Assimilation. The result of thought(s) will either be added to our base of understanding or rejected. Since all thoughts are connected, rejection means we have not taken enough time and effort to understand. Just like the fleas adapted to their new environment, organic life adapts to its environment. We are all caught up in the evolutionary process of thinking of ways to stay in balance. In fact, all organic life is subject to this process. But, how does a thought enter the mind in the first place?

"Cogito, ergo sum." DesCartes (I think, therefore I am.)

This quote is a great example of circuitous logic. Does DesCartes mean "I thinks, therefore I is?" If so, we are still stuck in trying to define "I." To some, it could mean "I think, therefore I am a thinker." What if he had said: "I feel, therefore I think, therefore I must exist?" He was actually involved in trying to prove the existence of a supreme being through logic when this statement was made. That definitely didn't happen. Logic prevailed.

Dr. Wayne Dyer was obviously a big fan of Public Television. His segment on the "Source" is quite interesting. He is addressing the source of our thoughts, it appears, and causes one to contemplate the question similarly to DesCartes' statement. Thought is caused by the dual nature of the wave/particle. To the imprisoned fleas, whatever makes sense matters and whatever matters, makes sense. The fault in that thinking is that there is no such thing as physical "matter." As Nikola Tesla accurately pointed out, everything we behold is energy in motion, vibrating in different frequencies. Newton accurately pointed out that there is no loss on energy in the universe and Einstein's Relativity equation says that energy equates to its observable forms. What if every thought we have is the Big Bang of our own Universe?

Understanding what we are entails understanding dual nature. Dual nature is evidenced not just in a myriad of instances, but in all instances. One of the oldest representations of this nature is the yin/yang symbol, created around three centuries BCE. In Chinese philosophy, yin and yang describes how opposite or contrary forces are complementary, interconnected, and interdependent in the natural world, and how they give rise to each other as they interrelate to one another. Yin cannot exist without Yang and vice versa. Also, Yin represents femininity and yang, masculinity. Carl Jung calls these traits anima and animus, respectively. All animals have both traits. They are what makes our male or female bodies. Equalizing both traits gives us androgynies, hermaphrodites or transgenders. They have both male and female sexual characteristics and organs; at birth an unambiguous assignment of male or female cannot be made.

Everything exists in our universe because of Dual Nature. This is called body/soul in a human being. We are all in a State of Being executing the Process of Becoming. The dual nature of Being/Becoming gives us consciousness. The process of becoming applies to all observable phenomena because energy is in a perpetual state of motion, interaction and evolution. There are no exceptions to this universal law except in the artificial mind we call Ego. Ego detests change and chooses to suppress the fact that everything executes the process of becoming something other than what it currently is.

We envision our universe because of the Time/Space duality. In general terms, our brain is equipped to interpret the waves of energy striking us as Frequency/Amplitude (Digital/Analog.) We have the same capability as an AM/FM radio, (Amplitude Modulation/Frequency Modulation.) We have the ability of focusing our thoughts to the frequencies/amplitudes that please us and/or "tuning out" those elements that "turn us off." If we allow egotism to tune out the truth, we will be living a lie.

Frequency allows us to imagine time and numbers while amplitude gives us dimension and location. The only time that exists in reality is NOW. There is no other time. We project past and future (before and after,) but they exist solely in our imagination. The only space that exists in reality is a point we call HERE. It has no dimension but contains all dimensions. As we wend our way from cradle to grave, we forever exist in the Here/Now and use our imagination to project There/Then. When our State of Being senses a discomfort in the Here/Now, we imagine a better There/Then and attempt to activate some Process of Becoming to regain balance in our State of Being. That is how we achieve all goals.

"Imagination is the beginning of creation. We imagine what we desire, we will what we imagine and at last create what we will." George Bernard Shaw

Politics and Religion take advantage of our bicameral brain. The apparent dichotomy actually addresses our frequency/amplitude. Politicians and the clergy create domesticated and obedient slaves to serve them while brainwashing the uninformed into believing they serve them. The brain is materialistic on the digital (frequency) side and idealistic on the analog (amplitude) side. Politics depend on money and status to motivate while religion uses the perfect life in heaven as the carrot.

"In our age there is no such thing as 'keeping out of politics.' All issues are political issues, and politics itself is a mass of lies, evasions, folly, hatred and schizophrenia." George Orwell

"All religion, my friend, is simply evolved out of fraud, fear, greed, imagination, and poetry." Edgar Allan Poe

Both politics and religion have extremes that define their schools of thought. They comprise the bipolarity of society. The duality in politics is the left/right (conservatism/liberalism) and religion follows suit with fundamentalism and Buddhism. Religion is normally defined as worshipping some imaginary supreme being. Buddhism is actually the absence of religion because there is no god in Buddhism. Buddhism is a philosophy (love of knowledge) that highlights kindness, beauty, compassion and unity. Today's religions and politics create untrue guilt, sin, and fear to manipulate the uninformed ego. There is no conflict between good and evil -- the conflict is between truth and untruth. The only way evil can exist is if we believe in it. It is religions that create hell on earth.

"The ideals which have always shone before me and filled me with the joy of living are goodness, beauty and truth. To make a goal of comfort and happiness has never appealed to me; a system of ethics built upon this basis would be sufficient only for a herd of cattle." Albert Einstein

When we seek to change our State of Being, we execute the Process of Becoming. In computer terms, the process of becoming is a System, Program or Application. All systems have three components: Input, Process and Output and all systems have to be connected to exist in reality. Output represents our imagined goals, Process represent the various methods to achieve those goals and Input defines the resources and talents that are required for the process to achieve a successful result. All activity on the planet (not only human beings) follows these same laws in goal achievement. It is only when the ignorant human ego makes decisions that we suffer consequences.

The problems on Mother Earth are caused by injecting faulty programs (schools of thought) into the memories of the ego. We are all programmed through indoctrination, propaganda, false beliefs and values, etc. to execute processes that benefit those who program our ego. The only way to return the planet to its perfect state of being is to shed all lies and rediscover our own perfection in the process. We have to become captains of our ship and masters of our fate, rather than slavishly obey artificial rules intended to serve a corrupt leadership.

"The dissenter is every human being at those moments of his life when he resigns momentarily from the herd and thinks for himself." Archibald MacLeish

"Nothing pains some people more than having to think." Dr. Martin Luther King, Jr.

The human ego has the unique ability to stop a thought and contemplate it. The cycle of thought processing goes through several stages -- Awareness, Focus, Analysis, Action and Adaption. The place to be while executing these steps is in our Corpus Callosum. That is the center and balance point of our consciousness. It can be had by meditation. It is our Creative Thinking Center. Ego has no control when we are in this meditative state. We will have achieved self-control. We will be able to change the perception of our universe by changing our thoughts. We are on the way to becoming a mystic.

Mystic: "A person who seeks by contemplation and self-surrender to obtain unity with or absorption into the absolute by the spiritual apprehension of truths that are beyond the intellect."

Through mysticism, we develop spiritual wisdom, expanded awareness and a sense of connectedness with everything and everyone around us, and, in the process, we become captains of our ship and masters of our fate. This state of mind is evidenced by the Toltec Spiritual Warrior, the Buddha of Buddhism, the Hindu yogi of hatha yoga, the Jesus (Christ Nature) of Christianity and the Sufi of Islam, as well as many other examples. Reaching this level of enlightenment necessitates total understanding of what we are. Everyone has the ability to find their mystical being, but few will make the effort to do so. The mystic lives in a perfect state of being and becomes oblivious to mundane human activities. He has risen above and beyond his animal body because he lives according to Natural Law.

The mystic can be likened to a Spiritual Warrior or bodhisattva in Buddhism. The term defines one who combats the universal enemy: self-ignorance (avidya), the ultimate source of suffering according to Buddhist philosophy. A heroic being with a brave mind and ethical impulse. Different from other paths, which focus on individual salvation, the spiritual warrior's only complete and right practice is that which compassionately helps other beings with wisdom. This is the Bodhisattva ideal (the "Buddha-in-waiting"), the spiritual warrior who resolves to attain buddhahood in order to liberate others. The term is also used generically in esotericism and self-help literature. Spiritual warrior, "illuminated heart and valiant one", "enlightenment hero", "one who aspires for enlightenment" or, "heroic being" has been defined as a bodhisattva.

Natural Law is that set of laws that is the working basis of all creation and without which no manifestation can occur and exist. It is universal in scope and manner of operation, simple and direct. Natural Law is always constructive even when it seems indisputably destructive. It is the expression or manifestation of Cosmic Energy and order that humanity is able to discern. There is no such thing as supernatural law. There is nothing more divine than nature, nothing super beyond the natural. The greatest of miracles are not the result of some supernatural law, but of natural law. The mystic has removed all vestiges of fantasy, indoctrination, false beliefs and false values and is synchronized and harmonized with the symphony of life.

Mystics do everything they can to cultivate and maintain four primary virtues: understanding, service, compassion, and love. These virtues all flow into one another and end up merging into a perfect unity and forming one entity. Willpower, perseverance, and trust are three further virtues that need to be manifested to achieve spiritual elevation. The choice is ours, for we have our free will.

"In practical living Illumination follows both Intuition and Idealism. Our intuition helps us to form a series of steps to climb. Each step in turn is an ideal; each ideal is more advanced, and more satisfying to our highest psychic self. An ideal may start with health, with personal well-being. Then it may advance to a consideration of the welfare of others, the service of society and then gradually broaden with greater understanding. The idealism prepares the consciousness for Illumination." Ralph M. Lewis

From childhood, we begin hiding our inner self away. We learn to adapt and survive in the outside world. Our families and peers teach us socially acceptable behavior. Our educational system teaches us the technical and social skills we need to sustain a material life. As adults, we are thrust into a society geared towards materialism and maintaining the status quo. Rarely, especially in the early formative years, are we taught inner development; with an emphasis on intuition, the subconscious mind, independent thinking, self-esteem, self-confidence, psychic or inner spiritual growth. The road to enlightenment is an arduous one, but is available to all. That road is not one of learning something new, but rather one of discovering what was always there.

Of the four primary values, understanding is utmost in importance for the simple reason that we cannot know others more than we understand ourselves. Performing service with compassion and love comes easily once we understand what we are.

The mystic who knows something of the inner light of consciousness is bound to be a little difficult to be absorbed; he is going to be an upsetting force. Most egos don't want to be disturbed, even though they may be in misery. They are in misery, but they are accustomed to the misery. And anybody who is not miserable looks like a stranger. He who has achieved self-control is the greatest stranger in the world; he does not seem to belong to anybody. No organization confines him, no community, no society nor nation. His very way of being is rebellious - not because he is fighting against anybody or anything, but because he has discovered his own true nature and is determined to live in accordance with it. He challenges us to be courageous enough to take responsibility for who and what we are and to live according to truth.

All of us need other people to learn from. We need the example and teaching of others who have done so before us, especially those who have gained insight into the nature of reality themselves. More broadly, "Mystic" refers to the people with whom we share our spiritual lives. We need the guidance of personal teachers who are further along the path than we are, and the support and friendship of other practitioners. This is very important because mysticism is not an abstract philosophy or creed; it is a way of approaching life and therefore it only has any meaning when it is embodied in people.

Moral rules and ascetic rites are not necessary for Enlightenment. Rules and rites exist in the realm of the ego and its animal instincts, not in the spiritual universe of the mystic. Attachment to sensual desire, creature comforts and selfish interests are no longer important. The attraction of conceit, selfishness and ego development is eliminated, along with ill will towards all. The mystic desires to live in the formless universe of Consciousness, Eternity and Infinity and the true Spirit of Living. He strives to achieve understanding and peace without restlessness.

"Personal transformation can and does have global effects. As we go, so goes the world, for the world is us. The revolution that will save the world is ultimately a personal one." Marianne Williamson

Taking responsibility for one's own life is something most people do not do. Governments and religions depend on servitude to maintain control over a population and do not want their slaves to think for themselves - their power would disappear if everyone woke up. They talk about education, but what is in our schools is training to create wage slaves. To educe means to "draw out" while politicians and clergy use schools to suppress and oppress uninformed egos. Our duty as parents is to teach our children HOW to learn, not what to learn. Unfortunately, most parents will inject their fears, prejudices, traditions and the like into the children's brains because they do not understand their own life.

"Education is not merely neglected many of our schools today, but is replaced to a great extent by ideological indoctrination." Thomas Sowell

Personality is analogous to ego. "Persona" means mask, or veil. Stage plays have dramatis personae as the cast to act as the scriptwriters decided. As Shakespeare pointed out, the world is a stage and we are all players on it. The ego has duality represented by the Jekyll/Hyde model. One side of the ego is constructive and creative while the other is destructive and reactive. Until we realize that we can only gain control of our lives by centering ourselves in the Corpus Callosum (between the hemispheres) can we begin to achieve Utopia. That is what meditation is intended to achieve.

The ego gets its consciousness from the five physical senses -- that is sight, hearing, touch, taste and smell. In the Rosicrucian study called "Mastery of Life," these senses are defined by the body's ability to differentiate the frequency and amplitude of "vibrations." The human body is a poor conductor of universal communication; eagles see better, dogs smell more, dolphins hear better, etc. That is one reason why using ego to make decisions is harmful -- it doesn't understand much of totality.

The human form, as all other forms, is comprised of atoms. These atoms come from Mother Earth and will be returned to her eventually. Each moment we live disseminates millions of atoms outward and we absorb millions of atoms in return. That is evolution in progress -- reshaping forms.

Each atom has electrons orbiting the nucleus. If we were able to collapse the electron orbits of Mother Earth, she would be the size of an average orange and the seven plus billion humans would easily be contained in a teaspoon. If we dig deeper into the structure of the atom, we eventually find the wave/particle nature of consciousness. The particle feels the wave and the wave thinks about the particle -- conscious thought is born.

When an electron orbits, it is impossible for it to complete an orbit and return to the exact spot it started because energy is always in motion. The orbit will create a circle or ellipse that will always be a bit off in replicating its path. That is probably why the value of PI will never come to a complete number. What this electronic orbit represents is a THOUGHT -- more accurately, a THOUGHT CYCLE. Since all things have atoms with electronic orbits that create thought cycles, this is the connection we have with the universe. There is no separateness.

In George Boole's "Laws of Thought," the ego mind identifies, categorizes, evaluates and prioritizes stimuli it encounters to decide whether or not to take action and, if it acts, what action is most appropriate for the existing circumstances. We internally vote on what is the most important thing for us to do every moment. You are deciding right now as to whether you will keep reading or go on to something you consider more important to you. All life is continually addressing its number one priority to act upon right here, right now and under the current circumstances. No exceptions. Boole's "Calculus of Logic" depicts how we reach decisions with formulaic definitions.

Ego functions

It is the end of the sixth day of creation and God has gathered all his angels and addresses the throng:

"Dear angels, we have worked wonders in these last six days. We have created the Universe with all its galaxies, stars, and solar systems and set them all in motion. Here on earth, we have created a paradise of wondrous beauty; mountains, oceans, rivers, forests and deserts along with plant and animal life galore. For these creations to be appreciated, I have created Man and appointed him steward of my work. Tomorrow will be a day of rest and, from now on, every seventh day will be a day of rest. (Cheers from the throng)

"There is one last thing I must do before we retire. Man has everything possible for him to enjoy life on the planet but needs motivation to explore and appreciate the beauty of my creation. I have decided to hide the secret of life from him and give him a yearning to find it. I need some suggestions for where I can hide it."

A voice from the rear of the gathering:

"Put it on top of the highest mountain, God."

"Not bad, but I have made Man intelligent and resourceful and he would probably find it before he has come to appreciate much of what I have wrought."

A voice closer in:

"Hide it at the bottom of the deepest ocean!"

"That's much better, but Man will be developing tools and ways of protecting his body when he explores and again find it too soon."

A cherub at God's knee:

"Why not put it where he'll never look?"

"Where would that be, little one?"

"Put it inside him."

Looking within oneself for the meaning of life is not a common exercise. Insight necessitates internal communication. We are constantly communicating with ourselves. Many people actually verbalize conversations with themselves aloud as they stroll in the park, cooking, while driving, or whatever. Who are the participants in those conversations and how are they related?

Sigmund Freud suggests that the Ego, Id and Superego comprise the psyche of human beings. These elements can be construed as the Trinity of Consciousness. Their relationship and interaction create the universe we envision and can be used to expand our insight.

EGO is the part of the mind that mediates between the conscious and the unconscious and is responsible for reality testing and a sense of personal identity. It evaluates perceptions to make decisions about the body's next action.

ID is the part of the mind in which innate instinctive impulses and primary processes are manifest. It is the natural "Operating System" that resides in all organic life, including Mother Earth.

SUPEREGO is the part of a person's mind that acts as a self-critical conscience, reflecting social standards learned from parents and teachers.

That trinity creates the PSYCHE - the human soul, mind, or spirit.

"The conscious mind may be compared to a fountain playing in the sun and falling back into the great subterranean pool of subconscious from which it rises." -- Sigmund Freud

(Joseph Campbell compared it to a wave on the ocean, momentarily rising as an individual and returning to its source.)

The three elements of our psyche mentioned above can be related to our brain. Freud's Ego can be defined as the Corpus Callosum; the Id resides in the right hemisphere and the Superego, the left. These are generalities to use in our analysis.

Babies are like clean slates that have all the necessary knowledge built in to sense their physical environment. Their sensors are tuned to monitor their "Comfort Zone" from their Id (animal instinct.) The response to an out-of-balance condition in their body is to cry for help. Their first "outside" relationship is usually with the responder that wants the child to stop crying. Babies contain much more knowledge than what allows them to interpret their senses, however. Using our insight to delve into this knowledge for understanding life should be the primary purpose of education. We should teach our babies how to learn, not what to learn.

From childhood, we get programmed, indoctrinated and domesticated. We learn to adapt and survive in the "outside" world. Our educational system teaches us the technical and social skills we need to sustain a material life which creates wage slaves to serve the Plutarchy. We need to start using our brain's ability for critical thinking and creativity to break through the self-created barriers of slavish thought.

Some have had a 'peak' experience, an ecstatic moment or a moment of greater understanding, when consciousness expanded. When this occurs, the integration between left brain (logical thinking) and right brain (intuitive feelings and emotions) is manifested in increased energy-flow between the two sides. This is thinking and feeling in a holistic and balanced way. It is a foretaste of an evolutionary jump for humanity - and in essence, what the so-called New Age is all about - a new level of maturity in mental development, an awakening.

By learning how to arouse the whole brain, selectively and at will, the mode of consciousness may be freely altered, appropriate to the task or situation - whether a crisis, making music, relaxing, mental arithmetic, brainstorming, or contemplating nature. In this new wide-awake consciousness, the world seems to be full of possibilities -- it possesses a strong sense of rediscovered meaning. This is nothing mystical. It is essentially ordinary consciousness, operating for once at its proper efficiency.

Dr. Jill Bolte-Taylor writes of such an experience in "Stroke of Insight" and has a seventeen-minute video on TED.com describing it. Her insight rid her of thirty-seven years of emotional baggage dumped on her by society. We all have the same opportunity.

"When you are inspired by some great purpose, some extraordinary project, all your thoughts break their bonds. Your mind transcends limitations, your consciousness expands in all directions and you find yourself in a new, great and wonderful world. Dormant forces, faculties and talents become alive and you discover yourself to be a greater person than you ever dreamed yourself to be." - Maharishi Patanjali

"We do not receive wisdom, we must discover it for ourselves, after a journey through the wilderness which no one else can make for us, which no one can spare us, for our wisdom is the point of view from which we come at last to regard the world." -- Marcel Proust

Wisdom is analogous to understanding. Babies are born wise before well-meaning adults transform them into domesticated animals, just like themselves. Only through insight can we return to our innocent wisdom and free ourselves from societal programming. It begins with taking total responsibility for what we behold.

"I no longer view the world in terms of unfortunate accidents or misfortunes. I know in my being that I influence it all, and now finding myself considering why I created a situation, rather than saying, "why me?" Dr. Wayne Dyer

We are normally born with five physical senses to experience our worldly travels. These senses provide input to the brain for evaluation and action (or inaction.) Each sense is "tuned in" to a specific range of vibrations that allows it to communicate its findings to our inner being. If we allow the ego to make comparisons or judgments of those findings, we will suffer consequences. Only our intuition will "feel" the truth of the stimuli we experience. Ego falls quite short in its ability to discern the connectivity of its observations because the senses provide only a tiny slice of what is actually there. Because of its stubborn and narcissistic insistence for seeing itself as separate and judgmental, it spoils the harmony and synchronicity of life itself.

Our five physical senses exist to maintain balance and staying alive. They tune in to the respective frequencies of the energy waves striking the body.

Smell. We need to breathe in oxygen to live. The composition in the air we take in is usually about 70 percent nitrogen, 21 percent oxygen and the rest is normally inert gases. We do not want to breathe potentially lethal gases like radon and natural gas.

Radon sensors are calibrated to the wave frequency that identifies its presence (smoke detectors fill a similar function when sensing the air content.) The utility company adds a garlicky smell to natural gas to alert us when a leak is endangering us. These sensors expand our ability to analyze the air we breathe.

Energy waves that attract us to what "smells good" include the barbeque, roses, perfume and fresh air. A sizzling steak has a very difficult aroma to ignore. A wine taster's nose is quite valuable in the success of a vineyard.

Taste. This sense is to prevent our Intake of poisonous food and water. It also allows us to ingest aliments that tastes "really good." Fast-food restaurants are experts at making their menu taste "really good," even though their nutritional value is questionable. There are many food critics who fancy themselves as epicures getting free meals to tell us what is good to eat – as if we couldn't make that decision ourselves.

Touch. What is a greater feeling than feeling a baby's cheek against our own? Touch tells us what is hard or soft and hot or cold. There is no better experience than human flesh touching human flesh in harmonious contact.

Hearing. If these words were to be read aloud to us, they would create images in our minds by vibrating the air molecules between the speaker and listener in patterns that are recognizable as human language(s). The speaker would inhale air and expel it while modifying the vibrations with vocal chords, tongue, teeth and lips to send energy that would vibrate the eardrum of the listener in patterns that create the images.

The difficulty in communicating verbally is that people attach different meaning to the same words. It is not what someone says that is important, rather what is understood by the recipient. If communication is the sending or receiving of a message than means the same to both sender and receiver, languages often fall short of that definition.

The language of music is one everyone understands. It appeals to our inner sense of harmony and balance and has existed since the dawn of man. (Picture a Neanderthal humming after a sexual encounter in the cave and gleefully striding out to gather food for his mate and children.) Many governments have been toppled by people singing a unifying song. "Imagine" is Utopia's anthem.

Sight. The minute segment of the electromagnetic spectrum we call visible light strikes our ocular rods and cones with waves of energy that create images in our minds. The narcissistic ego often ignores the fact that the spectrum is contained in everything and everyone. It defines a very narrow range of beauty by relating it to what appeals to the ego, rather than the spirit we all share.

We are all born perfect in the sense of containing the truth. That sense is Common Sense, sixth sense or intuition. From the moment we are born, the ego is subjected to indoctrination, propaganda, false beliefs and values, as well as fantasy, fiction and folklore, thereby eventually becoming a slave to others' thoughts. To return to our innate truth and gain the self-control we want, we must peel away all the vestiges of untruth -- like peeling an onion. Truth doesn't care about the ego's perspective. It will remain what it is. There is no conflict of good and evil; the real conflict is between truth and untruth.

Literacy has a huge impact on the size of an ego's universe. The higher our literacy skills, the greater the universe. A piece of knowledge is mere trivia until it finds its connection(s) in our overall knowledge base. A piece of a picture puzzle is meaningless until we find the corresponding shape in which it fits. It's easy to apprehend a new piece of information, but we must comprehend how and why it fits in our universal view for it to develop. It is comprehension that makes our universe grow. Without a high level of literacy, the puzzle will remain unsolved. Until the ego is motivated to remove its ignorance, it will remain a victim and a slave to others' thoughts and goals. There is a simple difference between ignorance and stupidity - Ignorance is not knowing and stupidity is refusing to comprehend.

Ego is very much like a gatekeeper to its perceived universe. Its job is to gather input from our physical senses and submit it to our true mind, but it has the ability to reject new information from entering if the information threatens its Comfort Zone. It does not like to change when it feels comfortable. If pressured, ego will activate its "fight or flight" reflex to relieve the pressure. The other option is to stay indifferent to the stimulus and simply do nothing.

Running away from truth and/or remaining as an obedient animal doesn't improve our perceived universe. It is when ego attempts to fight truth that we have the opportunity to improve. Those who feel stressed are merely resisting truth. It is impossible for truth to be defeated, but the conflict may allow the ego to recognize the faulty thoughts it had harbored. In the effort to prove itself right, the ego may "see the light" of truth.

There are numerous ways to be aware of when the ego is taking charge of our actions. Anger, greed, fear, lust, pride, vanity, dominance, and other selfish behaviors are ego traits and easily recognized (and/or manipulated) by the ruling class. Those traits indicate a lack of understanding. To remove any ego trait, we must fight to remove it by knowing why we exhibit it.

Plato's Cave

This writing by Plato is helpful in analyzing the ego:

Plato has Socrates describe a group of people who have lived chained to the wall of a cave all of their lives, facing a blank wall. The people watch shadows projected on the wall from objects passing in front of a fire behind them, and give names to these shadows. The shadows are the prisoners' reality. Socrates explains how the philosopher is like a prisoner who is freed from the cave and comes to understand that the shadows on the wall are not reality at all, for he can perceive the true form of reality rather than the manufactured reality that is the shadows seen by the prisoners. The inmates of this place do not even desire to leave their prison; for they know no better life. The prisoners manage to break their bonds one day, and discover that their reality was not what they thought it was. They discovered the sun, which Plato uses as an analogy for the fire that man cannot see behind. Like the fire that cast light on the walls of the cave, the human condition is forever bound to the impressions that are received through the senses.

Even if these interpretations (or, in Kantian terminology, intuitions) are an absurd misrepresentation of reality, we cannot somehow break free from the bonds of our human condition - we cannot free ourselves from phenomenal state just as the prisoners could not free themselves from their chains. If, however, we were to miraculously escape our bondage, we would find a world that we could not understand - the sun is incomprehensible for someone who has never seen it. In other words, we would encounter another "realm," a place incomprehensible because, theoretically, it is the source of a higher reality than the one we have always known; it is the realm of pure Form, pure fact.

Ziglar's flea jar is also similar to Pink Floyd's Wall (as in the album: "The Wall: by Roger Waters.) The songs are the depiction of a personal journey of building and eventually overcoming a self-made prison (Plato's Cave).

Self-Actualization

In 1949, Abraham Maslow published his Hierarchy of human needs. He intended to portray the motivation the ego uses to make its decisions. It classifies them by importance to the human ego.

1) Survival

2) Security

3) Social Acceptance

4) Self Esteem

5) Self Actualization

These have since been expanded by others into something like:

1)   Survival – Physiological

     a.   Homeostasis

          Natural Law dictates that balance of any form is necessary for existence.

     b.   Breathing

We must exchange carbon dioxide for oxygen to maintain natural balance

c.   Sleep

To replenish our body's oxygen supply and mend our wounds

d.   Water

To cleanse our internal organs and flush

e.   Food

Fuel to burn during our daily activities

f.   Excretion

Ridding ourselves of poisonous waste

These are listed in priority sequence. They constitute the Operating System requirements that all organic life is born with – including plants. Their intent is to stay in harmony and synchronicity with Mother Earth. After these priorities are met in humans, the actions we perform are all based upon societal and imagined values of our goals.

We are always involved with our Number One priority (Here/Now under the circumstances) of the scenario we occupy. If we do not like the scenario we occupy, we can change the circumstances within or move to a different scenario. We have to work within the system in order to change it. That entails understanding how and where the system is lacking. In technology, that is called debugging. This is the first rung in the ladder of understanding. All other so-called "needs" are actually ego "wants."

2)   Security – Safety

      a.   Body

      b.   Health

3)   Social Acceptance – Love and Belonging

A.   friendship

B.   family

C.   intimacy

After the above requirements are fulfilled, the ladder of understanding addresses finding the ego's value in society:

4)   Self Esteem - Social Stratification

A.   achievement

B.   confidence

C.   respect of others

D.   respect from others

E.   respect for oneself

Achievement breeds confidence and confidence breeds respect, but one's value for these behaviors is limited to which ism(s) they apply. If we are great racists within a group of racists, we may have those traits, but our thoughts will be far from being Utopian.

Confidence comes from experience and addressing life from a Utopian and mystical way. The dichotomy between confidence and insecurity defines character traits that separate us:

Confident   Insecure

Open Mind vs Closed Mind

Willing to learn vs Know-it-all

Gives compliments vs Seeks validation

Takes Responsibility vs Makes excuses

Acts on principles vs Whatever feels good

Admits mistakes vs Blames others

Positive vs Negative

Does not judge others vs Gossiping

Risk-taker vs Comfort zone seeker

Makes decisions vs Avoids decisions

Always learning and growing vs Stuck in routines and habits

It's not difficult to understand which side grows respect.

5)   Self Actualization

        a.   Morality

b.   Spontaneity

c.   Creativity

d.   Acceptance of truth

e.   Patience

f.   Transcendence

The above are all personality (ego) traits. They are not needs, only wants. The only way to achieve transcendence is to eliminate all wants. Characteristics of self-actualizers:

1)   They perceive reality efficiently and tolerate uncertainty

2)   Accept themselves and others for what they are

3)   Spontaneous in thought and action

4)   Problem-centered rather than self-centered

5)   Unusual sense of humor

6)   Able to look at life objectively

7)   Highly creative

8)   Resistant to enculturation, but not purposely unconventional

9)   Concerned for the welfare of humanity

10) Capable of deep appreciation of basic life-experience

11) Establish deep interpersonal relationship with few people

12) Peak experiences

13) Need for privacy

14) Democratic attitudes

15) Strong moral and ethical standards

The above capabilities exist in all of us, but few actually activate themselves regularly and consciously to live life accordingly. Daily behaviors need to change. Behaviors leading to self-actualization:

1) Experiencing life as a child with full absorption and concentration

2) Trying new things instead of sticking to safe paths

3) Listening to feelings instead of tradition, authority or the majority

4) Avoiding pretense and being honest

5) Having no fear of being unpopular

6) Taking responsibility and doing the best possible

7) Identifying defenses and giving them up

A large percentage of the world's population never gets past social acceptance. Many will attempt and fail and their ego will shove them back into that step. Those egos run back to their various support groups to lick their wounds and perhaps give up trying. We all have a perfect being waiting inside to be discovered. Regardless of whether we tell ourselves "I can" or "I can't," we're correct. We have to know that self-esteem is created by our belief and value systems and that we judge ourselves in accordance with those elements. It is not that we weren't born perfect, only that ego is faulty in its beliefs and values. Ego's ignorance makes it stop questioning its thoughts and actions and rely on others' programming instead. It can be called Beelzebub for the religiously inclined.

Building Understanding

Social stratification is normally visualized as levels of social standing or class. Many use money as a measurement stick to define the strata, but there are other definable social strata. We can define strata in terms of intellect, emotion, leadership and other elements. If we want to impact a progressive change for Mother Earth and her inhabitants, the most important social ladder to climb is Understanding. (Stop standing under the ladder in fear – walk to the other side and start climbing!).

There are only three elements to our perceived universe – Time, Space and Understanding. In general terms, the left hemisphere our brain receives waves of energy and segments those waves as frequency, thereby creating our concept of time and number. The right hemisphere receives the same waves, but interprets them as amplitude, thereby creating our concept of space and Point of View. Like an AM/FM (Amplitude Modulation and Frequency Modulation) radio receiving the very same energy waves, we tune into what we consider important and/or entertaining.

The kindred spirit that exists in all life resides forever in the time we call "Now" and the space we call "Here." Spiritually, it is always Here/Now, always has been and always will be. Death does not exist in the Here/Now.

From this Point of View, we project our thought energy outward (like a radar beacon) and receive the echo of those energy waves. If we sense something in that echo we do not like or understand, it is because we either sent out incomplete or incorrect thoughts, we are misreading the echo, or both. Truth, and truth only will clear up the messages. Of the three elements defining our universe (Time, Space, Understanding) we can only do better through better understanding.

In Utopia, competition is replaced by communication, collaboration and cooperation for the benefit and progress of the whole. There is no room for individual ownership, power or greed. The prevalent isms of a sane, safe and healthy society are anarchism, humanitarianism and communism working in concert.

After the basic needs of human existence are satisfied, most people desire kinship, freedom and love. Freedom of expression, freedom from fear, freedom of movement, understanding and growth underpin Utopian society. Children are regarded as seeds destined to blossom into their purpose for being rather than be trained to become wage slaves. Traditions, superstitions, false beliefs and values are replaced with the understanding that we are all threads in the fabric of Universal Consciousness. Development of the arts and sciences in young minds is the objective of education. To "educe" means to develop or make something appear. To access the power we all possess when connecting with the Universal Consciousness is the goal of Utopian education.

Utopians know that Mother Earth is the provider of our sustenance. Respect for our mother is a primary concern for all her inhabitants. These is no waste nor pollution in Utopia. There is no usage of her resources for the purpose of destruction, decadence and frivolity. The quality of life has nothing to do with material things or toys to occupy idle minds. There are no polluted streams or poisoned atmosphere in Utopia. Cities which have become like skin cancer upon her face are replaced with common sense, self-sustaining communities that harmonize with her Nature. These communities would be connected by technology that is available today. "Agrihoods" and other self-sustaining communities like Plant Chicago are popping up more and more.

Utopia is achievable without violence or coercion as Gandhi proved. It can be attained by the removal of false ideas and separatist isms. It will sprout when the gentry who support the ruling class turn their attention to those being ruled. After all, the only reason the ruling class has power is because we allow them to take ours.

Music has the ability to bring people and their thoughts together. The anthem of Utopia is John Lennon's song "Imagine." The message of the lyrics imply that the way to "live as one" is to eliminate the isms of organized religion, politics and money. It may be that Yoko's influence, probably based upon Eastern philosophy, had an impact on John. Buddhism is not a religion, but rather a philosophy. (Philosophy is the study of the fundamental nature of knowledge, reality, and existence, especially when considered as an academic discipline.) The Tao is the path to enlightenment and is analogous to the path to Utopia. The Taoists and Buddhists goal is Oneness, just like Lennon's Utopian lyrics.

The Cultural Ego

Traditions, religions, institutions, political blocs and the like are examples of Cultural Egos. If an individual rebels against an ism, all kinds of punishments can be meted out by the group. Laws are written and established to maintain adherence to these artificial schools of thought and appropriate punishment is defined when violated. Moses, Confucius, Mohammed and others attempted to give guidance to the members of their society. The Babylonian laws of Hammurabi are the probable cause for the Jewish scribes to include in the Bible as the Ten Commandments. The Sharia is another version. Those laws are rules to manage the ignorant and are only useful to the rulers.

Cultural egos are very difficult to change. That is because the individuals within them have little idea of what they could do by thinking "outside the box." Additionally, the reinforcement of the "group think" becomes powerful enough to overcome most individual thinking.

Society trains and domesticates its members. It is done by individual agreement of each member. It is done by propagating belief and tradition that once served to unify groups. We have the unique ability to stop a thought and think about it. To behold a thought and evaluate its meaning is the most powerful capability of human beings. To pass thought through the Corpus Callosum to the emotional hemisphere and gather meaning is a virtual miracle. In this age of constant belaboring by the cacophony of meaningless input, it is difficult to focus on what is truly important. We have to use this ability in order to change the path we have created. We have to prioritize our life by accepting what is important to each of us. We have to stop clicking on cultural icons to activate the apps that have been programmed into us.

We need more people to become leaders to create Utopia

Imagine yourself strolling in the woods on a bright, sunny day. The sun's rays form slivers of light peeking through the foliage and contribute to an overwhelming sense of well-being as you commune with nature. Up ahead, you notice a clearing -- a good place to sit and rest.

As you get nearer to the clearing, you notice what appears to be a vehicle of some sort. It doesn't resemble anything you know, so you edge closer to check it out. Just before you enter the clearing, you feel a hand on your shoulder that scares the beejeebers out of you. Spinning around, you are faced with a humanoid form unlike anything you have ever seen. Wordlessly, you hear a voice in your head: "Take me to your leader."

After the initial shock, you gather yourself and realize the alien is serious. He really wants to meet your leader. Who would that be?

The current crop of politicians comes to mind. Giving it some thought, you realize how embarrassing it would be to introduce this creature to any of them. The giants of industry are considered briefly and quickly dismissed because of their unending greed, hunger for power and corruption. The Queen of England comes to mind, but you don't consider her to be your leader. The Pope would be closer, but the way he dresses is really out of date. The Dalai Lama and his peaceful ways would probably make a better impression, but he doesn't have as many followers as he should. You hadn't actually thought about how difficult this request could be.

You ask yourself: "Who do I follow?"

After exhausting a sizable list of potential candidates, you eventually face the alien and say: "You're looking at him!"

The alien, again wordlessly, replies "That's the correct answer."

It is impossible to have peace in our life without taking responsibility for it. If we are willing to surrender our freedom to others in exchange for "security," we do not have freedom. If we are to sacrifice our time and effort to serve the corporate interests instead of dedicating ourselves to our neighbors and family, we are just a cog in the wheel of Fascism.

What do we really need to have a safe and joyful life? Our current leadership is surely ineffective when it comes to providing equality to its citizens. People are herded into manageable groups, like cattle driven into the slaughterhouse yards. Leaders hire "goons with guns" to protect themselves rather than the population. Surveillance systems are installed to remind us of Orwell's "1984," and politics mirror his "Animal Farm." Today's politicians are like the Morlocks feeding on the Eloi as depicted in H. G. Wells' "Time Machine." "Soylent Green" depicts how, because of crop shortages, nutrition is packaged into small bricks for consumption. Soylent Green is advertised as the latest and greatest way to get protein and nutrition. The protagonist eventually discovers that the primary ingredient is human cadavers.

Corporations run the world as shown in "Rollerball," and the military/industrial complex ravages the planet as described in "Avatar." Science Fiction has a way of becoming science fact. And yet, the population sleeps.

The majority of the population is not playing the same games as the leadership, although they do play many games. Play is the healthiest and happiest activity we can provide our babies, and our own childhood is re-experienced by playing with them. While most of us can be content with Little Leagues, board games, video games, and the like, the Big Boys play World Domination. There are very few players who can last long enough to create a New World Order. Despots and satraps are dispatched at will by the major bullies, idealistic resistance is squashed, and truth is hidden by the players by designating it "Top Secret." In "A few Good Men", Jack Nicholson is being grilled by Tom Cruise while on the witness stand:

Tom: "Tell us the truth!"

Jack: "You can't handle the truth!"

That's the unfortunate fact for most uninformed egos. They live in denial. When confronted with information that makes them face the truth, many people retreat into illusion and/or delusion rather than remove their ignorance. Many give up their thinking ability to bask in the warm glow of "someone will save me." Waiting for some imaginary friend to save us from our ignorance is not the way to create heaven on earth. There is no leadership in that attitude. Returning to Maslow's model, we see that, to reach Self-Actualization, we need to break through the Self-Esteem level, (where ego likes to live). There are definite traits of those who achieve that level.

Tolerance -- This quality is non-judgmental and accepts life for what it is. It is one of the defining traits of liberalism and progressive thought.

Spontaneity -- An almost eerie capability to do the right thing at the right time. It means allowing our true consciousness (gut-feel) to choose the best fork in the road.

Discernment -- Removing fables, fiction and fantasy to find truth. Politics and religion have done a superb job of removing critical thinking from the masses.

Wisdom -- Using knowledge and logic together to create better circumstances. Knowledge is only forgettable trivia until it is absorbed into a greater body of understanding.

Appreciation -- Knowing that simply being conscious is enough to be thankful. Nothing but consciousness is *needed* – everything else is a want.

Concern -- Commitment to the welfare of all living things. All life is connected – nurture all of it.

Inquisitive -- Needing to understand why things are as they are. Know WHY we do what we do.

Loving -- An all-encompassing compassion and kindness – unconditional love.

Some behaviors that can help reach Self-Actualization:

Concentration -- Living as a curious child to absorb as much meaning as possible from experience.

Exploration -- Finding new ways to achieve goals and expanding our understanding in the process.

Confidence -- Having no fear of being unpopular.

Honesty -- Knowing that the worst truth is better than the best lie.

Creativity -- Using the imagination to create a better situation.

Responsibility -- Realizing we create our own problems.

If we want to take the alien to our leader, we should look for those who exemplify the above traits. In the looking, we will find all of them within ourselves. We do not need politicians nor clergy to run our lives – they need us in order to survive.

These qualities are surely not exhibited in nonsensical tweets.

"Realizing that our actions, feelings and behavior are the result of our own images and beliefs gives us the level that psychology has always needed for changing personality."
Maxwell Maltz

Scientists are working on the Grand Unification Theory (GUT) in order to mathematically define the connections between the microcosm and the macrocosm of the observable universe. The terms needing definition are microcosm and macrocosm. If successful, the equations would prove the validity of Leonardo's "everything is connected," but only in the physicality of the forms. If GUT is the physical (hardware) definition, its dual nature necessitates a software definition. That software is Natural Law. In higher mathematics, there is no room for incorrect or incomplete thoughts when explaining truth. The primary purpose of scientific inquiry is to create PROOF.

The software of the universe is Natural Law. It can be referred to as the Grand Operating Design (GOD). It serves the same function as the operating system of a computer. Even as we sleep, our operating system exchanges carbon dioxide for oxygen, pumps blood through our circulatory system, digests food, etc.

Understanding that duality is inherent in all observable phenomena can be reached by equating human thought to the software in a computer. Hardware/software is equivalent to body/spirit. Quantum Mechanics proves the existence of the wave/particle duality with the same equation. Experiments have shown that, whenever a scientist thinks of a particular action while observing the behavior of a smashed atom, that imagined behavior occurs -- mind over matter, if you will.

The mind is obviously not physical, but metaphysical.

Metaphysics

Metaphysics is all about the intangible side of our existence. One of the best examples of a metaphysical experience is the one Dr. Jill Bolte-Taylor describes in her book: "Stroke of Insight." She also has a seventeen minute video on TED.com explaining her experience. She had a golf ball-sized tumor in the left hemisphere that prevented her ability to receive waves in terms of frequency. She could only envision her universe through the analog capability of her right hemisphere, thereby seeing the holistic totality of the intangible. She became an instant metaphysician.

"The first philosophy (Metaphysics) is universal and is exclusively concerned with primary substance. And here we will have the science to study that which is just as that which is, both in its essence and in the properties which, just as a thing that is, it has." (Aristotle, 340BC)

"Somebody who only reads newspapers and at best books of contemporary authors looks to me like an extremely near-sighted person who scorns eyeglasses. He is completely dependent on the prejudices and fashions of his times, since he never gets to see or hear anything else. And what a person thinks on his own without being stimulated by the thoughts and experiences of other people is even in the best case rather paltry and monotonous. There are

only a few enlightened people with a lucid mind and style and with good taste within a century. What has been preserved of their work belongs among the most precious possessions of mankind. We owe it to a few writers of antiquity (Plato, Aristotle, etc.) that the people in the Middle Ages could slowly extricate themselves from the superstitions and ignorance that had darkened life for more than half a millennium. Nothing is more needed to overcome the modernist's snobbishness." (Albert Einstein, 1954)

With respect to the responsibility of intellectuals, there are still other, equally disturbing questions. Intellectuals are in a position to expose the lies of governments, to analyze actions according to their causes and motives and often hidden intentions. In the Western world, at least, they have the power that comes from political liberty, from access to information and freedom of expression. For a privileged minority, Western democracy provides the leisure, the facilities, and the training to seek the truth lying hidden behind the veil of distortion and misrepresentation, ideology and class interest, through which the events of current history are presented to us. The responsibilities of intellectuals, then, are much deeper than what Macdonald calls the "responsibility of people," given the unique privileges that intellectuals enjoy.

Understanding metaphysics is essential to understanding our world. Physics and metaphysics combine to create the duality of consciousness. They are the Time/Space of Einstein, particle/wave of Quantum Mechanics, the body/soul of human beings and the left/right chambers of the brain. Metaphysics can be described as the "knowledge to be what the physical form appears to be." Nikola Tesla called it instinct, others call it intuition, yet others refer to it as Truth personified.

Metaphysics means "beyond physical." In other words, the form is not the essence of what we behold. Beyond the form is an essence that we could refer to as a bundle of Thoughts. Just like an acorn contains the thoughts to become an oak tree, our human DNA has the thoughts to become a full-grown human being. We can identify with our body as contained in a three-dimensional environment that can be compared to a fractal. Therein is what we interpret as our universe. All manifestations of thought exist within their own fractal universe. All fractal universes communicate their being and are connected to greater thoughts.

In our current form, additional dimensions are beyond the brain's capability to understand simply because it is hard wired to interpret the physical senses within the three dimensions. The metaphysical "we" can visualize the possibility of endless dimensions that consciousness can eventually explore. That is the realm of higher mathematics that Isaac Newton, Albert Einstein and many others have envisioned.

"Divine metaphysics, as revealed to spiritual understanding, shows clearly that all is Mind, and that mind is omnipotent, omnipresent and omniscient, that is – all power, everywhere and all truth. Hence all in reality is manifestation of Mind." Mary Baker Eddy, founder of Christian Science

Since our ego is insistent upon judging physical limitations, rather than accept the connectivity of all life, it must be put aside as the leader of our thoughts if we are to break through the strife we have caused ourselves. It is only through taking ego's control away from running our lives that we may unify our individual fractals and create a Utopian peace.

Noam Chomsky is a master of linguistics and proposes that language and grammar are inborn for all humans. Duality in normal language is expressed in words like Being, Matter, Sense and others. They can be used as nouns or verbs, creating linguistic duality. All observable phenomena must have dual nature to have existence.

"God is Supreme Being the verb, not the noun." R. Buckminster (Bucky) Fuller

This Fuller quote basically says that God is metaphysical. In order to exist in truth, God must have a physical nature as well. In Christian dogma, this is achieved by creating a Jesus to represent the missing half. This is usually enough to satisfy the requirements for that religion.

"If you want to control a population, give them a religion." Noam Chomsky

When Einstein refers to the snobbishness of the modernist, he is referring to the materialistic view of the ego structure. Smug and self-satisfied egos have no time for the plight of others. Conservatism, Fascism, Imperialism, etc., all stem from the left hemisphere (digital) of the brain. Depending upon the level of control and manipulation these isms have will determine the health (or illness) of the society. The balancing factors from the right hemisphere (analog) include love, compassion and cooperation. Unless leadership is founded on maintaining balance between Physics and Metaphysics, suffering will occur. Witness North Korean society

There are plenty of examples in the artistic world of out-of-balance societies. One of the more famous ones is depicted in George Orwell's "1984." (Kim Jong-Un must be an avid reader of that book.) Orwell is best remembered for his political commentary as a left-wing anti-totalitarian. As he explained in the essay "Why I Write" (1946), "Every line of serious work that I have written since 1936 has been written, directly or indirectly, against totalitarianism and for democratic socialism, as I understand it." To that end Orwell used his fiction as well as his journalism to defend his political convictions. He first achieved widespread acclaim with his fictional novella Animal Farm and cemented his place in history with the publication of Nineteen Eighty-Four shortly before his death.

In "The Time Machine," H. G. Wells describes a future society where the separation of society is portrayed by the Eloi and Morlocks. The innocent and playful Eloi are bred as domesticated animals to be used as a source of protein by the Morlocks. Whenever a siren is sounded, (much like the sounding of church bells on Sundays) the Eloi start marching like zombies towards an entrance that leads to the subterranean habitat of the Morlocks. After enough food has entered, the siren stops and the doors are closed.

When the protagonist (Wells) discovers his time machine has been moved into the entrance, he finds a way to the web of tunnels beneath the surface and discovers the purpose of the Eloi. He returns to the surface to rally the Eloi by waking them out of their stupor and eventually overcome the Morlocks.

Current society is separated into the Military/Industrial Complex versus Mother Nature – Morlocks against Eloi, representing Physical and Metaphysical. Probably the best movie to display this conflict is James Cameron's "Avatar."

Avatar Scenario

In 2154, humans have depleted Earth's natural resources, leading to a severe energy crisis. The Resources Development Administration (RDA for short) mines for a valuable mineral — unobtanium — on Pandora, a densely forested habitable moon orbiting the gas giant Polyphemus in the Alpha Centauri star system. Pandora, whose atmosphere is poisonous to humans, is inhabited by the Na'vi, a species of 10-foot tall (3.0 m), blue-skinned, sapient humanoids that live in harmony with nature and worship a mother goddess named Eywa.

To explore Pandora's biosphere, scientists use Na'vi-human hybrids called "avatars," operated by genetically matched humans; Jake Sully, a paraplegic former Marine, replaces his deceased identical twin brother as an operator of one. Dr. Grace Augustine, head of the Avatar Program, considers Sully an inadequate replacement but accepts his assignment as a bodyguard. While protecting the avatars of Grace and fellow scientist Dr. Norm Spellman as they collect biological data, Jake's avatar is attacked by a thanator and flees into the forest, where he is rescued by Neytiri, a female Na'vi. Witnessing an auspicious sign, she takes him to her clan, whereupon Neytiri's mother Mo'at, the clan's spiritual leader, orders her daughter to initiate Jake into their society.

Colonel Miles Quaritch, head of RDA's private security force, promises Jake that the company will restore his legs if he gathers information about the Na'vi and the clan's gathering place, a giant tree called Hometree, on grounds that it stands above the richest deposit of unobtanium in the area. When Grace learns of this, she transfers herself, Jake, and Norm to an outpost. Over the following three months, Jake grows to sympathize with the natives. After Jake is initiated into the tribe, he and Neytiri choose each other as mates, and soon afterward, Jake reveals his change of allegiance when he attempts to disable a bulldozer that threatens to destroy a sacred Na'vi site. When Quaritch shows a video recording of Jake's attack on the bulldozer to Administrator Parker Selfridge, and another in which Jake admits that the Na'vi will never abandon Hometree, Selfridge orders Hometree destroyed.

Despite Grace's argument that destroying Hometree could damage the biological neural network native to Pandora, Selfridge gives Jake and Grace one hour to convince the Na'vi to evacuate before commencing the attack. While trying to warn the Na'vi, Jake confesses to being a spy and the Na'vi take him and Grace captive. Seeing this, Quaritch's men destroy Hometree, killing Neytiri's father (the clan chief) and many others. Mo'at frees Jake and Grace, but they are detached from their avatars and *imprisoned by Quaritch's forces. Pilot Trudy Chacón, disgusted by Quaritch's brutality, carries them to Grace's outpost, but during the escape, Quaritch fires at them, hitting Grace.*

To regain the Na'vi's trust, Jake connects his mind to that of Toruk, a dragon-like predator feared and honored by the Na'vi. Jake finds the refugees at the sacred Tree of Souls and pleads with Mo'at to heal Grace. The clan attempts to transfer Grace from her human body into her avatar with the aid of the Tree of Souls, but she dies before the process can be completed.

Supported by the new chief Tsu'tey, who acts as Jake's translator, Jake speaks to unite the clan and tells them to gather all of the clans to battle against the RDA. Noticing the impending gathering, Quaritch organizes a pre-emptive strike against the Tree of Souls, believing that its destruction will demoralize the natives. On the eve of battle, Jake prays to Eywa, via a neural connection to the Tree of Souls, to intercede on behalf of the Na'vi.

During the subsequent battle, the Na'vi suffer heavy casualties, including Tsu'tey and Trudy; but are rescued when Pandoran wildlife unexpectedly join the attack and overwhelm the humans, which Neytiri interprets as Eywa's answer to Jake's prayer. Jake destroys a makeshift bomber before it can reach the Tree of Souls; Quaritch escapes from his own damaged aircraft, wearing an AMP suit and breaks open the avatar link unit containing Jake's human body, exposing it to Pandora's poisonous atmosphere. Quaritch prepares to slit the throat of Jake's avatar, but Neytiri kills Quaritch and saves Jake from suffocation.

With the exceptions of Jake, Norm and a select few others, all humans are expelled from Pandora and sent back to Earth, after which Jake is permanently transferred into his avatar with the aid of the Tree of Souls.

The metaphysical relationship of Pandora to its inhabitants (trees included) is the same as the relationship of Mother Earth to its creations, (us included.) When the Na'vi greet each other, they begin by saying "I see you," referring to the kindred metaphysical spirit that binds us all. Pandora is a planet that is in total balance of physical and metaphysical natures. It is only a matter of time before Mother Earth addresses the greed and power of the military/industrial complex that currently rules.

There have been societies on earth that seem analogous to the Na'vi, primarily the indigenous populations of the Western World and the Pacific Ocean island societies, as well as Australian aborigines. They were all in touch with their metaphysical nature and in synchronicity with Mother Earth. The quest for power and greed of the European invaders virtually destroyed their environment and their way of life. Cameron appears to have empathy for those victims.

"The earth does not belong to us; we belong to the earth." Chief Seattle

"The Europeans came and killed our people, decimated the buffalo and stole our lands. In return, they handed us a Bible and told us we were saved." Native American saying.

"When the power of love overcomes the love of power, we will have peace." Jimi Hendrix

Frequency

In computers, zeroes and ones replicate the wave and particle relationship. They are organized to mimic the schools of thought of the programmer. Surveillance systems do their dirty work by installing software that can watch and react to electronic stimuli, like getting a ticket for going through a red light. They are congealed thoughts of the Fascist governing mind. There is no consideration in this kind of digital universe for human love, kindness or compassion. The current leadership is doomed to fail unless it begins balancing itself with emotion to care for all life. Fascists may possess a high IQ, but they sorely lack EQ. They use only the left hemisphere (digital) side of their brain. If using the brain completely means having your wits about you, Fascists are half-wits.

New World Order

I am an immigrant. We moved to the United States to reunite my father with his mother and siblings living in Chicago. They had been separated 43 years. On March 28, 1955, after six days of wretched seasickness, I looked up from my regurgitation spot to see the Statue of Liberty looming in the distance. I couldn't take my eyes off her as we got nearer and nearer. My mother had to come and drag me back to our cabin to get ready to disembark.

Getting processed through Ellis Island takes time. None of us spoke English and we had to depend on the compassion and generosity of a stranger who knew how to help us. He was French and had undergone the process before. After processing was complete, he took us to a taxi stand and told the cabbie to take us to Grand Central Station for the rail trip to Chicago. He would not accept anything but verbal thanks. When we got to the station, the cabbie was caring enough to walk us to the proper platform after we got our tickets. He also refused anything but verbal thanks.

The train ride would take about twelve hours. For me, sleep was impossible; I didn't want to miss any second of this new adventure. Sleep was also difficult for my brothers and my mom because we hadn't eaten anything for many hours -- at least ten or twelve. A steward came into the car with a tray of sandwiches and goodies for the passengers to buy. Our family fortune consisted of two one hundred dollar bills that my mother had converted from francs on Ellis Island. When she offered the man one of the bills, he shook his head and said he didn't have enough change and began moving away. A man a couple of rows behind my mom saw this and called for the steward to return. He took four sandwiches from the tray, paid the man and handed the food to the four of us. Again, he refused anything but verbal thanks.

These three encounters in a strange country with total strangers anchored the following in my mind: "A stranger is simply a friend I never met before." They exemplify the true humanitarian spirit of the average American — something that has been bulldozed by the Fascist administration in Washington.

The following morning, we were reunited with my father and his brother Stanley at Union Station in Chicago. My life adventure was underway.

In 1955, the world population was about 2.8 billion. We have almost tripled that as of today. As I think about voting in November, it strikes me rather odd that nothing has been said about this troubling trend. If, in sixty years, that same trend occurs, the earth would have to support more than 23 billion people. Not likely -- at least with the current lifestyles.

The 1956 Federal election was a landslide for Eisenhower. His campaign was the first time I tasted politics, albeit at a very low level. I collected "I Like Ike" memorabilia and hoped for his reelection. By the time his second term was over, I had acclimated to my new country and really hated to see him go. One of the most memorable speeches he gave was upon his exit. By now, television had become a common household appliance and I can remember some of it. This excerpt is significant for this year's election:

"Our military organization today bears little relation to that known by any of my predecessors in peacetime, or indeed by the fighting men of World War II or Korea.

"Until the latest of our world conflicts, the United States had no armaments industry. American makers of plowshares could, with time and as required, make swords as well. But now we can no longer risk emergency improvisation of national defense; we have been compelled to create a permanent armaments industry of vast proportions. Added to this, three and a half million men and women are directly engaged in the defense establishment. We annually spend on military security more than the net income of all United States corporations.

"This conjunction of an immense military establishment and a large arms industry is new in the American experience. The total influence -- economic, political, and even spiritual -- is felt in every city, every State house, and every office of the Federal government. We recognize the imperative need for this development. Yet we must not fail to comprehend its grave implications. Our toil, resources and livelihood are all involved; so is the very structure of our society.

"In the councils of government, we must guard against the acquisition of unwarranted influence, whether sought or unsought, by the military/industrial complex. The potential for the disastrous rise of misplaced power exists and will persist.

"We must never let the weight of this combination endanger our liberties or democratic processes. We should take nothing for granted. Only an alert and knowledgeable citizenry can compel the proper meshing of the huge industrial and military machinery of defense with our peaceful methods and goals, so that security and liberty may prosper together."

James Cameron's "Avatar" depicts the madness of corporate greed and military might.

Ike was probably the last Republican president. Those who followed him as Republicans were only pretenders to the name. They were bought and paid for by those that Ike warned us about above. The last true Democrat was probably Lyndon Johnson. Civil rights instituted under his administration that were first forged under John Kennedy make that probable. A quote:

"The American city should be a collection of communities where every member has a right to belong. It should be a

place where every man feels safe on his streets and in the house of his friends. It should be a place where each individual's dignity and self-respect is strengthened by the respect and affection of his neighbors. It should be a place where each of us can find the satisfaction and warmth which comes from being a member of the community of man. This is what man sought at the dawn of civilization. It is what we seek today."...Lyndon B. Johnson

Jimmy Carter was a good president, but way, way too biblical. Many voters do not know about the Tripoli Treaty, signed by John Adams in 1797.

Excerpt:

"If, therefore, from the settlement of the Saxons to the introduction of Christianity among them, that system of religion could not be a part of the common law, because they were not yet Christians, and if, having their laws from that period to the close of the common law, we are all able to find among them no such act of adoption, we may safely affirm (though contradicted by all the judges and writers on earth) that Christianity neither is, nor ever was a part of the common law."

Article 11 states: "As the Government of the United States of America is not, in any sense, founded on the Christian religion; as it has in itself no character of enmity against the laws, religion, or tranquility of Mussulmen; and as the said States never entered into any war or act of hostility against any Mahometan nation, it is declared by the parties that no pretext arising from religious opinions shall ever produce an interruption of the harmony existing between the two countries."

There is little doubt that the founding fathers were not religious and could not have foreseen what the United States has become.

"Belief is the death of intelligence."...Robert Anton Wilson

"There is a plot in this country to enslave every man, woman and child. Before I leave this high and noble office, I intend to expose this plot." John F. Kennedy - seven days before his assassination.

John Kennedy was a unifying force for the youth of our country. He was firmly against the Vietnam War as well as the growing military/industrial complex and was assassinated because of it. Under his administration, the Peace Corps was born and grew to over three hundred thousand young men and women. Their mission was to help less fortunate countries develop self-sufficiency.

His brother, Robert, could have carried on the ideals, but was also assassinated before he could even celebrate earning the Democratic nomination for the presidency. Dr. Martin Luther King, Jr. was assassinated for similar reasons.

The sixties and seventies gave rise to much civil disobedience and protest against what our elected officials were doing. Hundreds of thousands of people would go to Washington, D.C. to protest how our country was being run. Bob Dylan probably sang it best:

"Come you masters of war

You that build the big guns

You that build the death planes

You that build all the bombs

You that hide behind walls

You that hide behind desks

I just want you to know

I can see through your masks

You that never done nothin'

But build to destroy

You play with my world

Like it's your little toy

You put a gun in my hand

And you hide from my eyes

And you turn and run farther

When the fast bullets fly

Like Judas of old

You lie and deceive

A world war can be won

You want me to believe

But I see through your eyes

And I see through your brain

Like I see through the water

That runs down my drain

You fasten all the triggers

For the others to fire

Then you sit back and watch

When the death count gets higher

You hide in your mansion

While the young people's blood

Flows out of their bodies

And is buried in the mud

You've thrown the worst fear

That can ever be hurled

Fear to bring children

Into the world

For threatening my baby

Unborn and unnamed

You ain't worth the blood

That runs in your veins

How much do I know

To talk out of turn

You might say that I'm young

You might say I'm unlearned

But there's one thing I know

Though I'm younger than you

That even Jesus would never

Forgive what you do

Let me ask you one question

Is your money that good?

Will it buy you forgiveness?

Do you think that it could?

I think you will find

When your death takes its toll

All the money you made

Will never buy back your soul

And I hope that you die

And your death'll come soon

I will follow your casket

By the pale afternoon

And I'll watch while you're lowered

Down to your deathbed

And I'll stand o'er your grave

'Til I'm sure that you're dead"

These lyrics have probably never crossed the reader's mind before, but they are an example of the mentality that the Fascist right wing wants to suppress. Today, complacency rules. We will see what November brings.

The power of Democracy

It's that time again. As the candidates for the presidential election gather their forces to wage battle for American minds, we can already see some attacks in progress. There will be billions of dollars spent to sway public opinion towards one side or the other -- money that could surely be used in more productive ways. The process is a version of a "Game of Thrones."

Most of the voting public has little knowledge of what government is about and happily participates in the process much like watching a spectator sport. Sides are chosen, cheering occurs when one side appears to be winning and polls are taken to decide what kind of message to broadcast for the opposing side to "score". Eventually, the chosen one is the least despicable to the most voters.

Jefferson, Franklin and the other founding fathers intentionally put "Novus Ordo Seclorum" (New World Order) on the Great Seal for a reason. Regardless of whether or not their primary philosophy came from Freemasonry, all the symbolism on both sides of the Great Seal carry deep meaning of their intent. It is most likely that the democracy they envisioned was inclusive of all citizens, even though slavery was still in effect. The political atmosphere in the United States today absolutely reeks of exclusivity.

If human beings were a thinking species, they would not need to be governed. There definitely are a number of independent thinkers, but they surely comprise a minority. This group, however, is the one that matters most to the candidates. Many of the voters already have placed their minds into a concrete shelter to prevent any information from entering and confusing them with facts. They will be ignored by the candidates because their votes are secure. How did we get to this state of affairs?

There are many ways to govern the uninformed. The United States purportedly is a democracy, but that is just a facade for what is really happening. The ideal form of government is to have no politicians and no state. That would be Utopia. The current form of world government is Oligarchy -- government by the few. The oligarchs have used Capitalism to amass their power and use the military/industrial complex to terrorize the population while they party. Eisenhower warned us of the military/industrial complex, but was generally ignored.

Another word for the existing government is plutocracy -- government by the rich. If we combine the two, we can coin a new word -- Plutarchy. The members are comprised of consortiums like the Koch brothers have formed. The

Koch Plutarchs gather twice annually to feed the coffers of the conservatives for the purpose of swaying uninformed minds into their camp. They are champions of disinformation and misinformation to serve their own best interests. One of their biggest concerns is unionization. They go through great lengths to divide and conquer. The last line of the Communist Manifesto is "Workers of the world, UNITE!" That would shake the Plutarchs to their boots. The surveillance systems implemented and continually being improved is a good sign of their fears.

Evidence of the Plutarchy's control seems to have started in the mid-nineteenth century. Fantastic discoveries and innovations began popping up all over the globe like a kind of evolution revolution. The power of the human mind was unleashed in such a way to cause consternation for the Plutarchy. They found a method to stem the tide by establishing the United States Patent Office in 1871.

Touted as a way to protect inventors from encroachment on their ideas, the USPO was actually intended to alert the Plutarchy of potentially dangerous threats to their control. Nikola Tesla was probably the best example of being victimized by this new process. When he first published his findings on how to provide free energy to everyone on earth, J. P. Morgan and others promptly pulled the rug from that goal by eliminating financial support to continue developing the idea.

Isaac Newton laid a scientific foundation that enabled future scientists to look at the world with new eyes and his works are the cornerstone of much development to follow. His "Mathematical Principles of Natural Philosophy" is nothing short of genius. His work on Optics and the creation of Calculus (Leibniz is accepted as a co-creator) proves his value to the modern world.

The eighteenth and nineteenth centuries were times of fantastic scientific discoveries and enlightened thinking. Many attempts to automate human functions occurred in history, but the first truly significant advances were made by Charles Babbage, George Boole and Ada Lovelace in the mid-1800s. Babbage was commissioned by the British government to create the Analytical Engine that arguably would have become the first computer, had it been finished. Ada Lovelace is considered by many to be the first programmer. George Boole contributed Boolean Logic that is contained in all software today. His "Laws of Thought" and "Calculus of Logic" are the foundation of modern computing. It wasn't until Alan Turing came into the picture in late 1930s and early 1940s that computers began using binary as the base for programming. The Z3, created by Konrad Zuse in 1941, started the revolution of computer evolution.

One of the greatest geniuses ever born was Nikola Tesla. His insight of how the universe functions is at the core of today's technology. His hundreds of patents were ignored and violated by Thomas Edison, Samuel Morse and others but Tesla never took offense or indicated resentment. Edison was an opportunistic marketer more than an inventor. There is no cell phone, television or computer that does not use Tesla's discoveries. They are all based upon his: "If you want to understand the universe, think in terms of Energy, Vibration and Frequency." That statement is the source of the digital age and virtual reality. Virtual reality is an artificial computer mind that can communicate with the human mind.

One of the first notables influenced by Newton was Franz Mesmer, the founder of hypnotherapy. His "animal magnetism" concept was used to heal a young woman of 27 from a horrible condition that caused convulsions and many other symptoms. She was instantly and completely healed. Phineas Parkhurst Quimby used the same technique to heal Mary Baker Eddy from debilitating illness. Eddy went on to write "Science and Health (with a key to the Scriptures)" that is the foundation of Christian Science.

From these monumental works came the creation of the Industrial Age. Fulton, Edison, Tesla and others used the science of their predecessors to create the basis for the military/industrial complex. As factories were being built, agrarian society slowly gave up its lands to become wage slaves. Promise of a better standard of living lured young minds to growing cities. Whereas settlers had to be creative jacks-of-all-trades to survive and use both sides of their brain, industrialization has reduced their natural abilities to become simple and hypnotized "human resources."

The twentieth century brought major advancements. The airplane, automobile, Einstein's Relativity and the introduction of automation moved the world faster and faster. The Atomic Age was born, along with all the paranoia associated with mass destruction. All elements were now available to control the human ego and its decision-making ability. The Plutarchy was now pulling the strings.

Inventions and discoveries that would erode the coffers of the Plutarchy were suppressed and discounted. Turning desert into farmland was quickly stifled; leaded gasoline lasted far more years than it should because the oil barons didn't want to spend money to clean up the air; Exxon/Mobil suppressed their findings that burning fossil fuel contributed to the global warming, etc. If someone in power would oppose such activity, they would be dispatched by assassins. John and Bobby Kennedy, Martin Luther King, John Lennon and others were never allowed to further humanity. The Plutarchy had plenty of cash to motivate the killers. If not cash, brainwashing could be used.

The best weapon the Plutarchy uses today against the population is the television. Other media like radio and newspapers are also used to some degree but "a picture is worth a thousand words" works quicker and better. When Newton Minow gave his speech "The Vast Wasteland," related to the usage of television, he was also ignored. TV has definitely become the best brainwashing tool of the Plutarchy. It will be used extensively in the election process. It is no accident that schedules on television are called "Programming" because that is what it does to the human ego. This has evolved into new and improved brainwashing techniques evident in smart phones and social media outlets.

The media are controlled by the Plutarchy, without a doubt. Rupert Murdoch, Disney, Fox and many others continually distract egos from the truth. Sports, entertainment, booze and sex also are made plentiful to prevent independent thoughts from sneaking into the system. The idea here is to keep uninformed minds so occupied with irrelevant goals that the true goal of the Plutarchy is never sought. Diversion, distraction and disinformation keep the herds from stampeding. Pro and con means for and against. If unifying the population is analogous to fusion, Fascists use con-fusion methods to divide and conquer.

It must be understood that all life is to be treasured. There is no life form that is "better than" or "worse than" any other life form. Human forms, tree forms, indeed, all forms are interconnected and interdependent. The culprit that screws up the soup is the artificial mind we know as EGO. All life is doing its best to express itself in the environment it occupies. The ego is targeted by the Plutarchy to maintain its death grip on uninformed minds. This is accomplished by understanding how the human brain makes decisions and giving it input that will guide the decision in the direction the Plutarchy desires. It is a form of hypnosis that would make Mesmer proud.

Egos under hypnosis do not realize they are hypnotized. They are aware of what they are doing, but they do not know the reason WHY they are doing it. When asked why they do what they do, they retreat into some babble to try and avoid embarrassment. They may quote what they heard or read or rely on cultural indoctrination to justify their decisions. They also may be so deeply hypnotized that they have lost their ability to think for themselves.

Egos are subjected to indoctrination, training and confusion. Education in the United States is primarily used to train wage slaves that can further the Plutarchy's interests. It appears that current curricula are sorely lacking in Music and the Arts. Cursive penmanship is disappearing in many schools. These elements are served by the brain's right hemisphere and this is the side that Plutarchs fear. Development of both hemispheres leads to effective and efficient decision-making. The digital side (left) communicates with the analog side (right) by traveling through the Corpus Callosum. We think about what we feel and feel what we think. If we all did that regularly, the Plutarchy would disappear.

Einstein's brain was dissected and found to contain a Corpus Callosum of huge proportions, no doubt from contemplating his Special Theory of Relativity. Expansion of the Corpus Callosum happens when we exercise it, just like our musculature improves with exercise. One of the best ways to do that is to meditate. If we seek a peaceful space and allow our true consciousness to express itself, we can cleanse ourselves of the ego's control. For the great majority of the population, this is no simple task.

Ego is a hugely persistent nag. Gimme, gimme, gimme is the constant cacophony of its unquenchable desire. And, once it has what it is nagging about, it seeks to hold onto it for dear life. Either that, or it becomes disenchanted with the worthless bauble it acquired and tosses it. Grasping, taking, holding for no other reason than to feel superior to other life forms. Ego is the only entity that wants more than it needs. That is why it is so susceptible to hypnotism. The Plutarchy is well aware of this.

Our universal consciousness is shared by all forms. Humans have animal bodies and will have inborn programming common to all animals. This is our Instinct.

We are born when sperm and egg unite and begin developing into our human form. The programming in the genes and memes of our parents and all previous ancestors is passed on to the body we will occupy while alive on Mother Earth. (Virtually all of us have Neanderthal traits.) This is our Intuition.

As we grow, we will acquire more and more atoms from Mother Earth to build a complete adult form. We will contain the same characteristics as Mother Earth herself. We are made of her dust and into her dust we shall return. The earth does not belong to wayward egos -- we all belong to Mother Earth.

The current infrastructure of world government uses technology to maintain control. Computers are extensions of the brain into the realm of zeroes and ones. Computers operate with a combination of hardware and software, and so do we. Computers can be digital or analog and so can we be. The Plutarchy uses communication systems extensively through computerization to manipulate uninformed and/or unthinking egos.

The brain operates much as an antenna that can both broadcast and receive vibrations of varying frequencies and amplitudes. As communication is received by the brain, messages contained in it will be examined first by frequency and then, amplitude. The left hemisphere handles the digital frequency and the right handles the analog amplitude. In the examination, communication through the Corpus Callosum occurs to create the MEANING of the message for the ego examining it. The longer the examination, the greater the meaning for the simple reason that all meaning is connected. The Plutarchy knows this.

Abraham Maslow's Hierarchy of Needs also applies to groups and government. His pyramid prioritizes these needs as: physiological, security, love/belonging, esteem and self-actualization. Current Fascism does not enter the Love/Belonging level.

Those who think their vote is worthless are absolutely correct in this political scenario. As long as egos are willing to be hypnotized, the Plutarchy will continue wielding their power. The current crop of Republican candidates is not republican. It is a Fascist extension of the Plutarchy. The Democratic side appears friendlier, but is still controlled by the Plutarchy. There is no one to blame. Everyone is doing the best they can under the circumstances. There are only three circumstances in living our lives: Time, space and understanding. Since it is always Here and Now, the only way to improve life is to address our understanding.

Plutarchs know that numbers and money strike the digital left hemisphere to create meaning and that meaning is evaluated in the Corpus Callosum to create an emotional reaction in the right hemisphere. Any ego that places the value of money above the value of life is sick, hypnotized or plain stupid. It is people who create money, not the other way around.

After the Second World War, the United States experienced a period of unparalleled growth and prosperity. Unified efforts by the citizenry had started a process of cooperation, community and general well-being for most. The "Baby Boom" indicates healthy relationships and promise of a good societal future.

After Eisenhower, things started changing a lot in the United States. One major reason, of course, was the proliferation of televisions throughout the country. After the Plutarchy dispatched the Kennedys and Martin Luther King, they had a relatively free rein to manage the population at will. Their wealth could now be grown by creating wars and bleeding wage slaves.

The Plutarchy Stratification

The pyramid above "Nova Ordo Seclorum" depicts an organized society in thirteen levels, relatively equal in rights and privileges. Thirteen is the number reflected in the obverse side of the Great Seal as stripes, arrows, olive branches, etc., presumably to depict the thirteen original states. Unfortunately, the existing society is more like a flattened disc with a very tiny percentage rising from its center.

We sometimes refer to the classes in society as Upper, Middle and Lower classes. Some would call them Nobility, Gentry and Hoi Polloi (the masses.) The Plutarchy at the top wields its influence downward to attempt to create their version of the New World Order. The primary purpose for exerting their influence is to create obedient servants to aid in reaching their goal. The Gentry (middle class) serves the Nobility (Plutarchy) with obedience and servitude. The Global Banking System and Plutarchic monopoly on what the media air are the two major tools for managing the servants. Threats and Fear of Retribution for disobedience also weighs heavily on the governed.

Level One

The plutarchy are the 20 or so families that own the majority of America's wealth and their corporate surrogates. The Rothschilds, Rockefellers, Oppenheimers, Bushes, Morgans and others are calling the shots. All politicians and clergy must be subservient to their wishes or be removed.

Level Two

The closer to the Plutarchy, the better the perks and privileges. Obedient lackeys that follow the philosophy of the New World Order will enjoy material wealth, opulence and decadence to their heart's content. The Koch brothers, maniacal politicians and others occupy this level.

Level Three

The Military/Industrial Complex that Eisenhower warned us about is alive and well. Both the military and corporations are structured as levels, as well. The Pentagon dictates how, where and when the generals and admirals will use their forces. The generals and admirals distribute the activities to the subordinate officers, down to those unfortunates who actually place their lives at risk to protect not the citizens, but the Plutarchy.

Corporations are similarly operated through boards of directors who are intertwined to support each other's production of materiel and money necessary to provide more power and money to the Plutarchy. Orders are passed to the CEO, CFO, CTO, etc. down to the Controller level to make the unfortunate employees do their bidding.

Beneath the Pentagon and the boards of directors are the officers who organize the people actually doing the dirty work. This is the Chain of Command. Each link in the chain gets access only to the information they need to fulfill their purpose, thereby creating confidential, secret and top secret designation for information that may expose the overall plan. (It would be interesting to find a "good" secret.)

Level Four

This level is the beneficiary of Trickle-down Theory or Reaganomics. There's not much trickling down these days. Between WWII and the eighties, the three levels of Nobility, Gentry and Hoi Polloi all improved their income and lifestyle. Reagan started the downward spiral of the middle class with that concept. What happened?

There has been an Occupy movement going on in the United States in which the protestors have styled themselves as the 99 percent who are protesting against the richest 1 percent who make their money though Financial Institutions, including the highly visible mega-banks. What the 99 percent fail to realize is that they are missing 9 percent of the target. The 1 percent had a major part in the ruination of our economy, the loss of our jobs, the loss of our houses, the loss of our life savings and the loss of our retirement. Where did it all go? Ask the 9 percent who serve the 1 percent. Therein lies the majority of blame for the robbing of the middle class and the further impoverishment of the "working class." Therein lie the people who used the 1-percenter's money to not only make more money for the 1 percent, but to make big bucks for themselves in the process.

The top 1 percent of our population owns 43 percent of the net worth of America. Also the upper half of this 1 percent own far more than the lower half of the 1 percent. In fact just 1/1000th) of the American population controls the majority of 43 percent of America's net worth. This comprises about 20 American Families who own about half of America's net worth. These families are identifiable, of course the Arkansas Waltons of Wal-Mart are in that 1/1000th are somewhere near the top, if not at the top. And, you know some of the other names, like Buffet, Gates and Koch. The point-one percenters are the ultra-rich and the rest of the 1 percent are the uber-rich.

The next 4 percent who own or control another 30 percent of our national wealth are the beneficiaries of the perks and privileges obedient servants receive. They together with the 1 percent control 73 percent (nearly three quarters) of our national wealth. The next 5 percent control 11 percent of America's net worth. (This 9 percent are known as the super-rich) This 9 percent (super-rich) plus the 1 percent (ultra-rich and uber-rich) comprise only 10 percent of America's population but own nearly 85 percent of the wealth in America. They own 90 percent of the privately owned stock, bonds, securities, commercial and residential real estate. Their name may not be on your deed, but they own the mega-corporations and mega-banks that own the debt instruments which represent the lien or mortgage on the real estate for our homes and our businesses,

However, there is another 10 percent (merely rich) who are the money makers for the highest 10 percent. These are the professionals, such as money managers, brokerage houses, banking executives, corporate executives, and a few lawyers who work for the owners and their corporations. These people invented the false value in the bundling of debt instruments which were assigned somewhat arbitrary worth based on the demand they created for even more debt instruments to bundle. It was these bundles of mortgages and other debt instruments that were sold to the mega-corporations owned by the top 1 percent and 9 percent. They called for more of these bundles or packages, which in turn created a demand for more of what went into the bundles; mortgages. This stimulated the money managers, investment bankers and brokers to create more debt instruments by encouraging looser/liberal lending and borrowing standards and, more importantly, to encourage lending on the equity that homeowners and commercial real estate owners had built up. This included small business owners and local owners of franchises who either bought or leased commercial space.

The banking industry went crazy giving out loans to homeowners based on a false increase in appraisal value that was not based on the actual value but more on the demand for the debt instruments (mortgages) which went into the bundles. The more of these mortgages that the money lenders wrote, the more fees there were for the brokers, the lender employees that wrote the loans, the secondary mortgage buyers who bought the loans and sold them to other investment banking sources who sold them in bundles to the investment funds and corporations owned by the 10 percent. And then you had the corporations, like AIG, who wrote insurance policies for the 10 percent which essentially guaranteed against losses in case the debt instruments in the bundles lost value. Then a combination of economic factors came together in a perfect storm which created higher fuel costs, higher food costs, higher credit card interest due to missed payments, higher payday loan interests due to missed or late payment, repossession of autos for late or missed payments, higher building material costs, higher delivery costs and the upward adjustment of interest payments in adjustable-rate mortgages (ARM).

Consumers, including homebuyers and small business owners prioritized payments, opting to pay for true necessities instead of on their loans. Mortgages became low priority, especially when adjusted to higher interest rates because of late payments. Business loans were neglected in favor of keeping the business going. Auto loans came next, student loans came next, and so on. Soon, home and auto repossessions and business failures went through the roof. Paying loans became the lowest priority. The chain reaction went up the pyramid driving down the value of houses and the value of the robbed equity that was represented in the debt instruments which drove down the price of the bundles which caused the top 10% to invoke the insurance they had purchased to protect themselves from just such a melt-down.

Remember the AIG meltdown and bailout. You and I paid for that and our children's children will continue to pay for it as well as the other bailouts of the Financial Industry - the very industry that created the crisis. But remember the Financial Industry was stimulated by the demand from the top 10 percent.

The net result of all this was even further loss of the value of the scraps the remaining 90 percent of us scrap over.

The middle class in America disappeared overnight. They are now part of the working class. Perhaps upper income working class, but slaves nonetheless. Some hung on to mortgages that were now underwater meaning the loans they owed amounted to much more than the house was now worth. They sacrificed other consumer spending to stay up with their mortgage, especially spending previously directed to small businesses, thus driving small businesses into either defaulting on commercial loans or being unable to pay their lease of commercial properties. This in turn caused the commercial space owners to default on their loans, which added another nail in the coffin.

The wealth of the wealthiest depends on those who serve them and those who work for wages that sustain the small businesses that sustain the corporate interest who either own them (franchises) or own the debt upon which small businesses are built. It is nothing less than ironic that we in America idolize the very rich and we have bought the myth that if we work hard enough we can be very rich too. That myth needs to be re-examined. It is the workers who create wealth for the wealthy while keeping just a small portion for ourselves. However, the wealthiest 10 percent (with the help of the 10 percent represented by the professionals) just reached in and robbed so many of us from what chance we might have of ever moving beyond being a wage earner, even us who are supposed to be the middle class. We may never become owners as the value was robbed out of what little we owned. The result is we are still sharecroppers or renters. The bulk of what we earn goes to the wealthy while we get just enough to sustain us to the next crop.

How can we not fear for the democracy that we are all taught is worth fighting for when the inequities of our economic conditions are so large and irresolvable? Even the ultra-rich and uber-rich know that the inequities are dangerous. Witness Warren Buffet imploring the Congress to "tax me more." The redistribution of wealth in a democracy has to be based on a tax that confiscates more of your wealth as you become wealthier. Our present tax system does not accomplish that goal at the upper end. Our present tax system confiscates more, as a percentage of wealth or earnings, from the wage earners, small businesses and salaried workers, not the merely-rich, super-rich, uber-rich and ultra-rich. The system is in turn enforced by the senators, congressmen, judges and political appointees who are sponsored by the wealthy.

Capitalism is a great method to control populations - give money to people to perform needed functions and take it back through taxes and living expenses. Those that perform complex functions are given more money and can keep some for themselves for entertainment and luxury. The banking system creates money by charging interest and uses its financial strength to support the military/industrial complex. Board members of mega-corporations communicate about how they can grow their power by cooperation and collusion. The result is world government by corporations like the one depicted in "Rollerball". James Cameron's "Avatar" depicts the lengths the military/industrial complex will go to further its unquenchable greed. Cameron's movie is an accurate portrayal of the current struggle on Mother Earth -- Plutarchy's insane greed using the military/industrial complex against Mother Nature. We need to change the culture from exclusivity to inclusivity.

The Plutarchy uses war to further its ambitions. The United States does have a defense budget, but rather an offense budget. All the current conflicts on the planet were started by the US in the name of national interest, but that is just a cover-up for the nefarious Plutarchy. They use patriotism, nationalism and separatism to gain support from the uninformed to exercise their imperialistic aims.

The Iraq War was touted to be a way to rid ourselves of the potential threat from Weapons of Mass Destruction (WMDs). The Bush administration staged the destruction of the twin towers in New York to rally support from the gullible. There is no structural engineer of even limited capabilities that would agree that those structures could come crashing down in a few minutes from the impact of the airliners. Likewise, if the Pentagon was hit by an aircraft, how did the wreckage disappear and why did the CIA confiscate the camera from the establishment across the road?

The activities related to mobilizing the Gestapo provides a training ground for new technology and weaponry and maintains a satisfactory level of paranoia among the hoi polloi. They appeal to the emotional side of the uneducated by glorifying fallen or existing "heroes" to quell dissension, for the most part.

"He who joyfully marches to music rank and file has already earned my contempt. He has been given a large brain by mistake since, for him, the spinal cord would suffice. This disgrace to civilization should be done with at once. Heroism on command, how violently I hate all this, how despicable and ignoble war is; I would rather be torn to shreds than be part of so base an action. It is my conviction that killing under the cloak of war is nothing but an act of murder." Albert Einstein

Service Revolution

The Industrial Revolution that created wealth and opportunity for many Americans morphed into the Service Revolution made possible by the advent of the computer. The United States moved from a manufacturing power to a service industry. Cheap labor in other countries to produce material and materiel were seen as a great method to transform create a service industry here. Who is being served is the burning question.

The Matrix is a fair depiction of how the Plutarchy's "reality" is controlled and managed. That reality is geared to maintaining subjugation of its members.

In the United States and other countries, the service industry has become the servitude industry. Global corporations and military might are the watchdogs that assure obedience or orchestrate reprisals using the trickle-down method. Power is passed down the chain of command by using dollars. The closer to the top, the more dollars you get (if you remain obedient).

The corporate brain uses the same concept as human brains to manage the corporate "body." Incorporation means "creating a body" and, although it is imaginary, many think it is real. All systems work that same way; all systems are interconnected, and corporations are no exception. However, the base unit of corporations is not the dollar -- it is the employee. Executives would have us think otherwise, but that is the fact.

The corporate body has a number of departments to maintain its existence. These are equivalent to the internal organs in our own body. The heart pumps blood through our arteries and veins to maintain our organs just as the General Ledger pumps dollars into departments. The Income Statement reflects activities similar to our own "To

Do" list. The brain directs actions within the structure per the directives of the board of directors, etc.

Mother Earth and the rest of the Universe operate under two laws: Balance and Sequence. If an out-of-balance condition is communicated to the Universal mind, it activates a correcting sequence to regain balance. That's it! There is no more mystery about how the universe works. Every other consciousness within the universe must follow these two laws or become extinct.

Corporations maintain a Balance Sheet and an Income Statement to replicate the Universal Laws of balance and sequence in the corporate body. The activities required to keep the corporate body alive are given numerical values (dollars) to go from one annual statement to the next. When the board of directors meet at year-end, they allocate dollars to functions they perceive as necessary by issuing a Budget for dollar distribution to the various departments (organs) for the creation of a better annual statement. Excess profits are distributed to investors as dividends to thank them for their mindless support of the Plutarchy.

Governments work the same way. The slave masters use the global banking system to funnel dollars into various corrals around the globe to maintain some semblance of order. When that order is threatened, send in the Gestapo to depose the disobedient. The United States modifies its Offense Budget to start wars in efforts to maintain specific corrals.

This matrix of control is based upon the relationship of the individual to the dollar. A dollar bill is a symbol of power and is actually a symbol of human effort. It is not what it is that matters to its holder, it is what it does. Winning the lottery means **freedom** to the winner. The desire for freedom is what the Plutarchy manipulates to have us do their bidding. This may be the plot that John Kennedy was assassinated for understanding. The service industry has become the Servitude Industry.

The global banking system is the greatest Ponzi scheme ever devised. The National Debt is an illusion. What it truly represents is the human effort the Plutarchy has stolen from society – they have the money to pay it off, if they choose.

Banks are in place to store dollars captured from witless individuals to create more money for the slave masters. Insurance companies exist for the purpose or protecting money for the same group. Pharmaceuticals spread fear of various symptoms to syphon money from an ignorant populace and perhaps inject "stupid pills" into their bodies. Panic and paranoia are rampant over a few thousand cases of the flu while millions of Somalians are starving to death. Get your flu shot before you wake up and realize your natural immune system and a healthy lifestyle is the best prevention for disease.

It is the servitude of the gentry that the Plutarchy seeks.

All systems work the same way and all systems are interconnected and interdependent. As Da Vinci said: "Learn to see. Everything is connected." If this is true, then we all are connected to whatever else we are able to discern. Connected by WHAT? Our own thoughts.

In attending a stage play, if we are to enjoy the performance, we are asked to "suspend our disbelief." In order to accept any new discovery within ourselves, we must do the same. The truth lives in all its forms, no doubt. The true consciousness knows how to maintain the form we occupy, as well as all forms it occupies. When the ego sleeps, our bodily functions are maintained by the Universal Balance and Sequence laws. When the ego and its body arise from sleep, the world's ills are roused, as well.

The Green Party

There needs to be a transitional period on the path to Utopia from the current system. There need not be a physical revolution or endless protests that achieve nothing. We simply need to extricate ourselves from servitude. A potential starting point is to adopt the Green Party mission statement:

1.   Grassroots Democracy

All human beings must be allowed a say in decisions that affect their lives; no one should be subject to the will of another. We work to improve public participation in every aspect of government and seek to ensure that our public representatives are fully accountable to the people who elect them. We also work to create new types of political organizations that expand the process of participatory democracy by directly including citizens in decision-making.

2.   Social Justice and Equal Opportunity

As a matter of right, all persons must have the opportunity to benefit equally from the resources afforded us by society and the environment. We must consciously confront in ourselves, our organizations, and society at large, any discrimination by race, class, gender, sexual orientation, age, nationality, religion, or physical or mental ability that denies fair treatment and equal justice under the law.

3.   Ecological Wisdom

Human societies must function with the understanding that we are part of nature, not separate from nature. We must maintain an ecological balance and live within the ecological and resource limits of our communities and our planet. We support a sustainable society that utilizes resources in such a way that future generations will benefit and not suffer from the practices of our generation. To this end we must practice agriculture that replenishes the soil, move to an energy-efficient economy, and live in ways that respect the integrity of natural systems.

4.   Non-Violence

It is essential that we develop effective alternatives to society's current patterns of violence. We will work to demilitarize and eliminate weapons of mass destruction, without being naive about the intentions of other governments. We recognize the need for self-defense and the defense of others who are in danger. We promote non-violent methods to oppose practices and policies with which we disagree, and will guide our actions toward lasting personal, community and global peace.

5.   Decentralization

Centralization of wealth and power contributes to social and economic injustice, environmental destruction, and militarization. We seek a restructuring of social, political and economic institutions away from a system controlled by and mostly benefiting the powerful few, to a democratic, less bureaucratic system. Decision-making should, as much as possible, remain at the individual and local level, while assuring that civil rights are protected for all.

6.   Community-Based Economics

We support redesigning our work structures to encourage employee ownership and workplace democracy. We support developing new economic activities and institutions that allow us to use technology in ways that are humane, freeing, ecological, and responsive and accountable to communities. We support establishing a form of basic economic security open to all. We call for moving beyond the narrow 'job ethic' to new definitions of 'work,' 'jobs' and 'income' in a cooperative and democratic economy. We support restructuring our patterns of income distribution to reflect the wealth created by those outside the formal monetary economy – those who take responsibility for parenting, housekeeping, home gardens, community volunteer work, and the like. We support restricting the size and concentrated power of corporations without discouraging superior efficiency or technological innovation.

7.   Feminism and Gender Equity

We have inherited a social system based on male domination of politics and economics. We call for the replacement of the cultural ethics of domination and control with cooperative ways of interacting that respect differences of opinion and gender. Human values such as gender equity, interpersonal responsibility, and honesty must be developed with moral conscience. We recognize that the processes for determining our decisions and actions are just as important as achieving the outcomes we want.

8.   Respect for Diversity

We believe it is important to value cultural, ethnic, racial, sexual, religious and spiritual diversity, and to promote the development of respectful relationships across the human spectrum. We believe that the many diverse elements of society should be reflected in our organizations and decision-making bodies, and we support the leadership of people who have been traditionally closed out of leadership roles. We encourage respect for all life forms, and increased attention to the preservation of biodiversity.

9.   Personal and Global Responsibility

We encourage individuals to act to improve their personal wellbeing and, at the same time, to enhance ecological balance and social harmony. We seek to join with people and organizations around the world to foster peace, economic justice, and the health of the planet.

10.   Future Focus and Sustainability

Our actions and policies should be motivated by long-term goals. We seek to protect valuable natural resources, safely disposing of or 'unmaking' all waste we create, while developing a sustainable economics that does not depend on continual expansion for survival. We must counterbalance the drive for short-term profits by assuring that economic development, new technologies, and fiscal policies are responsible to future generations who will inherit the results of our actions. We must make the quality of all lives, rather than open-ended economic growth, the focus of future thinking and policy.

The Green Party objectives are universal in their inclusion, not only for the United States, but for all countries. They are virtually perfect for unifying humanity. The founding fathers were pretty sharp. The three branches were intentionally designed as "Checks and Balances" and "Separation of Powers." Unfortunately, today's political environment does not reflect a working model. Racism, evangelism, sexism and downright hatred are evident in every corner of the country. The media are bought and paid for by corporate warmongers to broadcast lies and sugar-coated hope pills. Rupert Murdoch, Koch brothers, Disney, Pharmaceuticals, General Dynamics, General Electric, Dow Chemical, Monsanto, DuPont, the Rothschilds, BankAmerica, Chase, and numerous others all take part in bamboozling the public. They are the power regardless of administration. For the United States to return to a democracy, everyone must get involved.

"A world community can exist only with world communication, which means something more than extensive short-wave facilities scattered; about the globe. It means common understanding, a common tradition, common ideas, and common ideals." Robert M. Hutchins

The political system in the U.S. has two major parties -- democrats and republicans. Efforts have been made to break up this unholy marriage but failed. They use the "Divide and conquer" principle to maintain power and brainwash the population. Liberals are normally identified as democrats and conservatives are referred to as republican. They comprise the Left and Right Wings of an airplane that doesn't go anywhere. We the people are sitting in the cabin, arguing about whose point of view is right while the politicians have a drunken barbecue party on their respective wings. We need a good pilot to get us off the tarmac and into a better future.

The Green Party is the answer to breaking up the corruption. Many states are trying to keep them from federal elections for no other reason that they are gaining support from many disgruntled voters.

The above objectives are echoed to some degree by the Sierra Club. (Michael Bloomberg donated one hundred million dollars to this organization to help it stop coal-burning energy.)

Sierra Club Strategic Plan Overarching Visionary Goals:

Goal #1:

Achieve ambitious and just climate solutions

Solve the climate crisis in a way that protects the environment and also is enduring, fair, and equitable

Strategies:

- Transition to 100 percent clean energy.

- Maximize energy efficiency across all sectors, including transportation, urban design, and land use.

- Return greenhouse gas concentrations to a safe level below 350 ppm.

- Address non-energy emissions such as agriculture and methane.

- Protect and rebuild the capacity of forests and other lands to absorb excess carbon dioxide and provide more robust climate resilience through supporting biodiversity and natural system functions.

Goal #2:

Explore, enjoy and protect our nation's lands, waters and wildlife

Steward our natural resources to safeguard them for present and future generations.

Strategies:

- Protect and restore wildlands and waterways to provide large and connected habitats in all ecosystems that will withstand climate change, and also provide suitable habitat for the protection and restoration of rare and endangered species.

- Defend our wild heritage, onshore and offshore, from extractive energy development. Put an end to damaging mining, logging, and other highly disruptive resource exploitation practices.

•   Protect our air, water, land, and communities from pollution. Promote environmentally sensitive land use and urban design to minimize sprawl, provide a healthy environment for all, and minimize resource use.

•   Ensure that all who live in the United States have access to natural areas, including in or near their communities, as well as the opportunity to experience the natural world through Sierra Club outings or in other ways.

Goal #3:

Engage and support a broad, diverse, inclusive and powerful movement

Attract and empower a base of supporters and activists strong enough to challenge the status quo and accomplish our ambitious programmatic goals.

Strategies:

• Engage the public, civil society, the business community, and other partners who share our values.

• Lead in diversifying the environmental movement to reflect the demographics of our society.

• Have the clout to influence public perception and public officials on our core issues, and to elect and hold accountable environmentally committed leaders at all levels of government.

• Help our activists, local communities and allies win on the environmental issues most important to them. Engage in strategic alliances on broader issues if this can help further environmental causes and remain consistent with our values.

Goal #4:

Become an ever stronger, high-performance organization

Function as a high-performance environmental organization by building on our legacy and embracing innovation.

Strategies:

- Build powerful, capable, diverse, and inclusive volunteer leadership nationally and in every state and major metropolitan area. Diversify the staff at all levels and develop and support within all staff clearly defined values, leadership, and core competencies to excel in their field. Build a strong partnership and mutual respect between volunteers and staff.

- Foster an organizational culture that promotes results, accountability, learning, transparency, and good governance.

- Enhance the democratic and grassroots nature of the Sierra Club in a manner that balances centralized and decentralized power, on-the-ground and online mobilizing, and bottom-up, top down decision-making.

- Maximize the effectiveness of our campaigns at the local, state, national and international levels. Leverage all of our capacities, including communications, digital strategies, policy, organizing, and legal.

Goal #5:

Ensure our financial strength and sustainability

Ensure that the Sierra Club and its entities have a combination of diverse, secure, sustainable, and flexible funding that will enable us to:

• Win on our priority work and, where feasible, leverage our resources to help our movement allies win, too.

• Adapt to change as new opportunities and challenges arise.

• Invest in organizational capacity.

• Ensure that all of our chapters and groups have the financial resources and opportunities to succeed.

Aspiration Fund

If all adherents to the above goals would take action against the Plutarchy by transferring their accounts from the big banks, insurance companies, oil stocks, pharmaceutical stocks and all other non-green entities, a huge message would be heard by the Plutarchy.

Not only would your finances improve by joining this Fund and banking with them, but your children and grandchildren would enjoy a healthier and safer future.

Change is Necessary

Most people do not like change but in the next decade humanity is going to experience a rapid change unlike any ever seen before. We are in a transformative period. We have just started a new millennium. During this time during the last millennium, we were in the dark ages. The phrase "Think globally, act locally" has never been more important.

There are three forces at work which will completely change humanity.

First there is a flow to global. We are now in the nation-state period. All that is left is the planet-state. Everything is going to become global. As younger generations come to power, they are not going to have the same loyalties and ties to nation and corporation that their parents and grandparents had.

Second, everything is flowing to the individual. This is because we are being given more and more choices in every single part of our life. This causes power to flow from the producer to the consumer and from the institution to the individual. Just 30 or 40 years ago we had access to just two newspapers or three television stations for our information. Now with the internet we have access to unlimited information and therefore unlimited choice.

Third, all of humanity is being connected electronically. This is empowering the individual. This is giving leverage to third world countries. They can connect and compete just as any other nation. There are over 5 billion cell phone subscribers. There is no time or distance limiting human communication. Place has been eliminated in human connection. It does not matter where you are. This will cause upheavals in dictatorships. The people can see and connect past the rule and propaganda of the dictator.

We are moving from structure to nets. We don't need to work in a big high rise corporate building. We can work anywhere we have a computer. We can connect to anyone from almost anywhere in the world.

This gives us two realities. We have our physical reality and now we have a screen reality. The screen reality is just as important as the physical reality. Power is no longer in the hands of institutions who advertise to tell you what to buy, what to do, and how to be. Power is now in the individual. You influence those you are connected to on the web.

We are moving from physical to non-physical. Just consider money. Money is now mostly just a figure on a computer screen. Institutions are going to have to change their form if they want to stay current and compete financially. If they don't they will not survive. Most people are still stuck in twentieth century thinking and are not able to see the change coming. This is why so many things (especially with our government) are not working.

Everything changes. Just look back on your life and see how much the world has changed already. Within the next 10 years it is highly likely our entire world will be under one government. So many things are pointing in that direction.

The other choice is to create Utopia. This is an incredible time to be alive. How did we get to this point? A review:

Virtually everyone on the planet uses technology or is subjugated by it. The seeds of today's technological capabilities were sown a few hundred years ago. Blaise Pascal was a forerunner of computerization when he developed a method to help his father do his accounting work faster, thereby allowing them to spend more time together. Many were based on Isaac Newton's work. (Along with Leibnitz, he is credited with creating Calculus and wrote Principia and Opticks.) These are probably the major building blocks for supporting the technological revolution. Albert Einstein certainly gave Newton credit as the driving force for his Special Theory of Relativity.

All containers of intelligence use an Operating System to do their magic. In simplistic terms, this system must be capable of communicating in whatever environment the container exists. It is patterned after our own innate operating system and resides in all manifestations of FORM. Every object we perceive is in-FORM-ation and contains the intelligence to be what it is -- including us. Another fact is that ALL forms are interdependent and interconnected to create one Universe. There is no "outside." What we envision as human beings is what our human ego is willing to understand and can only be "seen" in our own mind.

Our innate operating system "knows" how to maintain homeostasis in our body. Even while we sleep, it pumps blood through our circulatory system, exchanges carbon dioxide for oxygen, wakes us when we need to go to the bathroom, etc. When we feel the need to purge, we activate an application to swing our legs off the bed, walk to the bathroom, purge and return to bed - we execute the "go to the bathroom" app. Everything we do in our waking state is an execution of one app or another. So it is with all containers of intelligence, whether they be kangaroos, giraffes, etc. -- or computers. Our operating system is instinctual and natural while our human apps are learned and arbitrary.

Every system is identical in the way it works and all systems are interconnected. There is no possibility of an "independent" system, including the human system. Only the human ego attempts to separate and differentiate itself from its universe.

All systems use INPUT to produce OUTPUT with a PROCESS. We eat various foods (input) to produce energy, body building blocks and waste (output) and assign that process to our digestive system. We intake air (input) so that oxygen can cause carbon molecules to "burn" and provide energy (output) to move our carcass while expelling carbon dioxide (output) to feed the trees using the process of our respiratory system. Each system we use for bodily survival has an engine we call "organ" and the sum total of these systems represent the human organism.

The five physical senses of the human body have been replicated in computers. This has given rise to the proliferation of surveillance systems and the birth of Big Brother. Privacy is a word in its final death throes. There are sensors to mimic a digital overseer for virtually every human activity. Automated speeding tickets and red light violations are common. Taking a picture of your check and sending the image to the bank's computer allows for instant deposit into your account, etc. Some electronic eyes can actually "remember" faces in a crowd. In fact, sensors have been developed that far exceed the capability of the human senses. Space probes billions of miles away provide information for scientists to examine, for example.

Communication systems have benefited tremendously by computerization. To be able to speak to someone across the world on a smart phone and even see their faces through Skype is nothing short of miraculous. Take a bow, Tesla. To have access to knowledge by simply saying "OK, Google" is a fantastic capability. That is the power all Utopians have. When everyone has access to the same knowledge base, we can "live as one."

Vibrations are replicated in a computer using strings of zeros and ones. When we use voice recognition in calling the local utility company, its computer is receiving our words in patterns of zeros and ones that enable it to compare our voice to its inbuilt dictionary. Then, it will consult its vocabulary and grammar to attempt avoiding human intervention in handling our request. It becomes a translator of vibrations between man and machine.

If Einstein's revelation that energy is the only element that creates forms and Newton's Law that no energy is lost in the universe is true, we can begin visualizing a holistic and totally connected universe in a state of constant change and transformation. What separates the various manifestations we are able to observe in our human form is based upon the frequencies of their vibrations. (In the "Mastery of Life" course offered by the Rosicrucians, the frequencies for each of our physical senses are outlined in detail.) Is technology the tool we can use to transform this universe? Indeed it is.

After Einstein's Special Theory of Relativity came Quantum Physics and Quantum Mechanics. This led to the scientists' discovery of the dual nature of the wave/particle. One startling discovery was that, while observing the behavior of the wave/particle, it would act according to what the experimenter was thinking - mind over matter, if you will.

The wave/particle is analogous to zero and one. Just as the wave/particle duality is the source of our consciousness, the zero/one is the source of computer consciousness. This fact is what will allow Utopians to tame technology and make it our slave.

The basic unit of today's computer capability is the **bit**. All automated functions are performed by its ability to sense when a bit is on or off. This allows for stringing thoughts in a linear fashion to achieve an objective. We are entering the age of Quantum Computers.

Quantum computers use a **qubit** as their basic unit. Rather than a two-dimensional approach, it is a three-dimensional concept. We exist in three-dimensional "MindSpace". The development of quantum computers is a huge advancement to enable Utopia.

Utopian Anthem

"Imagine" - Interpreted

John Lennon's vision in this song is what prompted me to write this book and how we can bring the ideals to life.

Imagine there's no heaven

It's easy if you try

No hell below us

Above us only sky

If we all stand on the equator for twenty four hours and continually look from horizon to horizon, we will have a better idea of "heaven." We're in it. Hell has no place in heaven; it only exists in the uninformed minds of the religious. The only thing that creates the idea of Hell is our own ignorance of the truth. The materialistic mind we call the ego, if not understood, will create imaginary creatures we call Satan, Beelzebub or Lucifer. Only truth exists.

"The only evil is Ignorance." Socrates.

Our spiritual self exists in the eternal and infinite dimension of Here/Now. There is no such thing as past and future, except what our minds project. Each night, the material mind dies and is resurrected when we awaken. During our sleep, the "Mind that never sleeps" keeps our hearts beating and lungs pumping, etc. Living in the moment according to Tolle's "The Power of Now" will allow us to regain our creative power. We imagine what our day will be like as we stir from our sleep and create it as we go. If we all work to make this day a better one for each other, we're on the right path.

Political borders are like corrals for the various herds the Plutarchy maintains. They are artificial lines that cannot be seen from space and exist only in the uneducated mind. Mavericks who try for freedom are seen as rebels that won't follow the dictates of the despots put in place to watch the herds. Violent force, propaganda, imperialism, patriotism and indoctrination are the tools used to try and maintain "peace" within each corral.

Nothing to kill or die for

And no religion too

Karl Marx said it best: "Religion is the opiate of the masses." Truly, addiction to a system of belief is much like heroin or cocaine addiction. Whether the addiction is to a book or a set of behaviors that others can mimic, it is addiction nonetheless. All beliefs are assumptions, not truth. Einstein has a view on Buddhism:

"Buddhism has the characteristics of what would be expected in a cosmic religion for the future: It transcends a personal God, avoids dogmas and theology; it covers both the natural and spiritual; and it is based on a religious sense aspiring from the experience of all things, natural and spiritual, as a meaningful unity." Albert Einstein

"Those who would believe absurdities can be made to commit atrocities." Voltaire.

Most devout folks are great neighbors and community participants. The Bible and Koran give them a common thread to unite and take care of each other. That is surely desirable in a Utopian society. However, credit for goodness, compassion and humanitarianism need not be assigned to an imaginary friend. Traditional religions were intended to control societal behavior more than gain spiritual insight. Spirituality is not achieved by separating oneself from some "Supreme Being." It is achieved by understanding Being as the Supreme enlightenment.

Imagine all the people

Living life in peace...

Many hope for World Peace, but do nothing. An occasional pang of discomfort occurs when we see the atrocities being committed by our military/Industrial complex, but that usually lasts only a short while. After that, we're just "too busy" to be peaceful.

You may say I'm a dreamer

But I'm not the only one

I hope someday you'll join us

And the world will be as one

There are dozens, if not hundreds of websites leading to world unity, but we must find a way to open the corrals without causing stampedes.

Imagine no possessions

I wonder if you can

Anyone who thinks he or she "owns" something is foolish. We may get license from our local overlord to use something for a while, but that's it. People who are obsessed with gathering material or money for some future purpose are only fooling themselves. Those who think they own something are actually being owned by the objects they think they have.

No need for greed or hunger

A brotherhood of man

The planet can provide food for everyone, even in this overpopulated condition. However, greedy commercial interests who provide without considering keeping the planet in balance are causing long-term pains for our children and grandchildren.

Imagine all the people

Sharing all the world...

The corrals are temporary. Just because the Plutarchy posts some goons with guns at the borders doesn't mean they will stay. Prejudice, jealousy, greed and ignorance will eventually die, not people.

You may say I'm a dreamer

But I'm not the only one

I hope someday you'll join us

And the world will live as one

Standardizing thoughts to be based on truth alone is difficult. Mass media feeds little minds with pap and propaganda and are rigidly censored to present candy-coated crap for easy digestion. Rupert Murdoch, Clear Channel, Disney, Time-Warner, etc. want to make sure the truth stays as hidden as possible. The natives get restless unless they are repeatedly told they are in good hands.

"Living as one" means "of the same mind," not necessarily living exactly the same way. There are preferences in each of us that can be addressed individually. The Golden Rule is the one that can create the same mindset. We can be addicted to that thought. Groups can create their own individual corrals and be with like-minded communities, as long as they do not negatively impact neighbors.

Our first responsibility is to help each other, but not at the expense of destroying the planet in the process. Commercial interests are so hungry for money that the methods used to provide for two billion people are still being used to provide for seven billion people. The one-eyed hypnotist we call television prods people to buy useless junk they cannot afford nor have any need for. Cutting down rain forests, raping the ocean wildlife, polluting our air and water for the purpose of providing unneeded goods and services is insane.

The place is here and the time is now. That is the state of being we will forever be. What we activate today is the Process of Becoming - coming to be some other state of being. If we do not adjust our priorities to ensure that what is important comes first, it will take longer to achieve. It will happen. We have the tools. Let's teach our youth how to use them so that they can create a future based on truth.

Epilog

In August 1995, Cognitor, Inc. was founded by this author and Paul T. I met Paul at some function in Chicago. We began talking about our experiences and he found out how long I had been selling software. Our conversation led to his request for me to accompany him to a presentation he had scheduled with Purdue University. He was trying to get a consulting gig there and wanted me to critique his presentation. I agreed.

He had created software that he called "Slice and Dice"; and his presentation of the capabilities of this software could not possibly be understood by the average person. When he was describing how it worked during his presentation, I saw the potential. On the drive back to Chicago, we discussed the meeting:

"Paul, you have created an artificial ego!"

"What do you mean, John?"

"Slice and Dice works exactly as the human decision process works, Paul."

We spent the next six or seven hours exchanging views and understanding until we decided to establish Cognitor, Inc. and rename the software "Cogitator" -- ergo my screen name. It means thinker, and that is what the software does. The company name was chosen because it is my Rosicrucian name. Cognitor means "defender." We were way ahead of our time. Few could grasp the meaning.

In 2007, I self-published "The Mind -- User Manual" with Author House in an effort to revive Cognitor. That was my first (albeit sophomoric) attempt at communicating my epiphany.

When I experienced my epiphany on February 6, 1982, I was both euphoric and petrified. I felt as though I had fallen into a river of understanding and didn't know how to swim. From that day, I have struggled to find words that can delve deep into consciousness and help others find that same stream of thought. Why? Because it is the "follow your bliss" that Joseph Campbell suggests we should all do. When I connect with others on the path to awakening, it makes all my swimming worth the effort. It is my "Reason for being."

All of us regard the universe we create from our individual and peculiar point of view. How we describe and explain our view to others is based upon language and action. My newly acquired view was overwhelming. How could I share this view with others? I would have to study and research to create the best possible communication possible. I will spare you the details of the dozens of books and thousands of hours I have dedicated to forging a meaningful message.

My focus turned from WHO I am to WHAT I am. That wasn't hard to do because my epiphany destroyed all egoistic tendencies. (Thank you, Ego, for stepping aside and letting me back into the driver seat.) Ego is meant to be a navigator for our meanderings and could no longer tell me where to go without my permission. My life wasn't all about knee-jerk reactions to stimuli before this, but a large part certainly had been.

I tried to spend as much time as possible ruminating about communication and why we do what we do. However, there were still bills to pay and other distractions to tend to. Having been exposed to some twenty years of experience in systems analysis, five or so years selling high-level executives in the Fortune 500, I had enough value to be hired for a two year stint in Saudi Arabia. Getting away from my comfort zone and submitting myself to another culture shock (my first was coming to the United States when I was ten) would allow me to grow. I also took a 45-day tour of the world that further opened my view. It helped clear my mind and steel my resolve.

When I returned to the US, I again dived into my stream of thought and felt more comfortable swimming in it. At times, I simply floated and contemplated my eventual destination. I did not know where I wanted my river to go yet. I thought about that day in February that had created my epiphany. It was after a class created by Wilson Learning -- Counselor Selling. This was a highly-advanced sales course that went deep into psychology and interaction during the sales cycle. I had noticed that the class did not have an accurate depiction of the process so I contacted Larry Wilson. At the time, Larry was attempting to define and create a Corporate Brain. I had a pretty solid idea as to how that could be done. After we spoke on the phone for some minutes, he invited me to his Pecos River Learning Center at his expense.

The Pecos River Learning Center is located about thirty-five miles north of Santa Fe, New Mexico. Larry had acquired about ten thousand acres to create this playground. He had given me a free pass to his "Ropes Course" of three days' duration.

Taos and Santa Fe are both artist meccas, primarily because of the incredible pure light that painters love. After New York and Los Angeles, Santa Fe sells the most art. (The town had about seven thousand residents at the time.) When I woke up the first morning on the ranch and walked outside in the brisk, fresh air and looked to the sky,

I understood why artists love this place. Clarity of light could never be better defined.

The "Ropes Course" is three days of breaking down the stubborn ego, aimed primarily at stodgy corporate executives. We were blindfolded and led by the elbow through rocky hills, made to fall backward from a six-foot platform into the arms of our comrades, climb a rock wall that necessitated having to let go of footholds to reach the top, etc. All activities intended to engender trust in others and remove egotistic behaviors in the process. There were group meetings as well to discuss our feelings and interact about our shared experiences.

It wasn't until the last day that Larry and I got to meet. I presented my case, and he stopped me much before I reached the conclusion to call his entire staff into the meeting room for them to hear what I had to say. That's when I knew my stream was going in the right direction.

I still had not defined as much of the stream to myself as I wanted. I spent three years studying the Rosicrucian "Mastery of Life" course, read more books and continually forged a better understanding of me. "Time, Space and Knowledge" by Tartang Tulku was one meaningful book that gave me further insight. I made a mental note to change the word "Knowledge" to "Understanding" because a piece of knowledge is mere trivia unless it gets assimilated into our base of understanding. It led me into studies of the brain and how we build our universe or, at least, our view of that universe. I finally reached the point where I could not see anything "wrong" in my view, save when my ego took control of the wheel. I learned how to calmly put it aside and return it to the navigator position. That's when I turned my attention to the current human condition.

If I can do it, everyone can do it. It takes time and attention. It takes commitment and understanding. It necessitates an open mind and a willingness to change and understand more. It means the Comfort Zone must be vacated. It involves becoming a truth-seeker.

Being human is a fantastic gift. There is no other creature we know of that has the range of capabilities and potential we have (maybe dolphins.) There are many traps humans fall into on the way to enlightenment, though. One of the most dangerous is habit. Another is action without thought -- (the Pavlov dog response or knee-jerk reaction.) Another is the herd instinct that groups us and insulates us from interacting with other groups or individuals "Birds of a feather..."

My first attempt at understanding was aimed at duality. I knew that wave/particle, yin/yang, frequency/amplitude, one/zero and many other analogies meant the same thing to me. No form can be perceived or exist without this duality. Form following function or function creating form is the chicken and egg paradox to me. How does this understanding apply to groups?

We are social animals. We want to feel we "belong." Many of us will do anything to "fit in" the social circle we want to be with, sometimes sacrificing our true purpose. We want to love and be loved from the moment we are born and perhaps before that. In creating these circles, however, we may encounter values and beliefs that exclude others. There is a myriad of values and beliefs that cannot possibly be true, but many people simply "go along with the flow." My stream of thought doesn't flow that way. There are no values nor beliefs in it. I either know or do not know. What I know is founded in truth, and what I don't know, I research until I can incorporate it into my base of understanding. No assumptions of ego are allowed to wade into my stream. When someone says: "I believe," it means "I don't understand!"

Social stratification occurs because of levels of understanding. Maslow's Hierarchy of Needs depicts these levels (and have been expanded by others.) Truth is, we have no needs other than consciousness – other so-called needs are only wants or desires. It is what we want that drives the economic system, not what we need. These unnecessary and egotistical wants are despoiling Mother Earth. As I've written in other essays, we do not need oil -- we need clean water and clean air; we need love and compassion, not atomic weapons; we need to share this planet, not assign ownership of pieces of it to the chosen few. It seems that the chosen few are leading this world into oblivion. We need new leadership for the masses unwilling or incapable of seeing this greater view.

The current lords and masters have many ways to have us spend money that they can put into their coffers. (A recent study stated that the richest eighty-five people on earth have as much wealth as the bottom 3.2 billion people.) That appears to denote inequality. How do they maintain control over the minds of the unfortunate and the disenfranchised? Why is there no outcry and revolution to depose these people and end this unfair and cruel treatment? The answer is lack of understanding to some degree, but more importantly, it is the inaction of those who could take the reins away from the oligarchs and plutocrats. Oligarchy is government by the few and plutocracy is government by the rich. I have taken it upon myself to coin a new word for the next revised version of the dictionary -- Plutarchy.

Government means to rule or influence others to perform behaviors according to a set of laws or agreements. Religion is a form of government. The Constitution of the United States is the set of laws and agreements establishing acceptable behaviors in society. The Bible and Koran, etc. do the same thing. One appeals to the material sense while the other affects the spiritual sense. This is how politics and religion govern the masses. If Gutenberg used his printing press to publish the achievements of Socrates, Plato and Aristotle rather than the fiction, folklore and fantasy of the Bible and Koran, the Dark Ages would never have occurred and this world would already be Utopia.

Logical Thinking

When I first started writing COBOL code, I became enamored with the IF/THEN statement. Simply put, it is the decision point for what the program should process next -- "IF value X is greater than value Y, THEN do this..." One aspect of this powerful decision-making tool is that I could "nest" multiple IF/THENs to make more complex decisions -- "IF this condition AND IF this condition OR IF this condition, THEN, THEN, THEN..." I still use this concept to analyze any new information I receive. This is how I connect my existing base of understanding to new information. It is how I reached my current State of Being. I am an information processor evolving by understanding -- I am a Being in the Process of Becoming a greater Being through understanding. We all are.

I started studying communication, linguistics and semantics to find better ways of stating my view. English is my second language; computer languages follow. Nine months after arriving in the States not speaking a word of English, I came in second in the school spelling bee. I even surprised myself. The significance of this result was not that I did it, but that I learned the language from the dictionary. Having to go through the mental gymnastics from French to English and English to French gleaned much more meaning from words than most native-born people.

We receive all communication through our five physical senses. The communication is felt through vibrations that carry both frequency and amplitude. The vibrations created by these words are felt by your eyes and interpreted as the image I want you to contemplate. Your brain has two hemispheres. The left interprets frequency of vibrations and the right, dimension of amplitude. If I have verbally painted the image I have in my mind properly, you will build that image in yours. We will have successfully communicated.

Love and compassion are created in the right hemisphere of our brain, not the heart. The heart is just another organ for the brain to monitor. That hemisphere is the door that religion enters to govern the believers. The left hemisphere processes the values of material society, primarily defined by politics while the right hemisphere's emotional capability is manipulated by religion(s). We need to know who is gaining entry to our mind and why.

Cogitator is very similar to Alexa, the voice-operated convenience of the tech-savvy millennials. Everyone in the world, regardless of language, could have access to Cogitator's knowledge bases to maintain balance for themselves, their community and the world of Utopia.

Cogitator

There are many technical terms that can be confusing to the average person. This is normally referred to as "shop talk" by those involved in whatever specialty they work. In the description of Cogitator, there are a number of terms that need at least some familiarity to grasp its operation.

Artificial Intelligence

"Artificial" means: *made or produced by human beings rather than occurring naturally, especially as a copy of something natural.* It is the source of the word "art" which suggests the depiction of some form of reality by an art-ist.

"Intelligence" means: *the ability to acquire and apply knowledge and skills.* This is the innate ability all organic life uses to maintain the necessary balance for survival. It cannot be artificial. The artificial part of artificial intelligence is KNOWLEDGE.

Knowledge

Knowledge is Facts, information, and skills acquired through experience or education; the theoretical or practical understanding of a subject. The experience it creates in an individual becomes a "scenario" that can be re-**membered** as a memory or meme. (The members of an experience are recalled to reproduce the scenario in our mind.) A meme is a single element of a system of behavior.

Creating the scenario necessitates understanding various aspects of knowledge. They include knowledge of:

What

When

Where

Why

How

Who

These are all requirements for creating a human scenario in a computer and can be stored in a Knowledge Base to be linked to related experiences. The knowledge base becomes a **translator** and **communication facilitator** for use by human beings. When successfully communicated between people, experience is **shared meaningful context**. "Context" is: *the circumstances that form the setting for an event, statement, or idea, and in terms of which it can be fully understood.*

Common Sense

The cornerstone of common sense is the FACT. Cogitator does not use assumption or belief in the construction of knowledge bases. Every element must have a connection to every other element and all elements must pass the test of truth and logic. Whenever it learns from human interaction, it adapts and updates its knowledge base(s).

As it "learns," Cogitator will occasionally perform a Merge/Purge routine. This is analogous to humans ridding their mind of trivia which had been incorporated into their life experience and creating a higher level of understanding – (move up a rung on the understanding ladder.) Once beliefs and assumptions are removed from a human mind, the climb up the understanding ladder picks up speed.

Accessing the knowledge base allows users to develop their heuristic prowess. Heuristics means enabling a person to discover or learn something for themselves. It is said that experience is the best teacher but, in truth, it is the ONLY teacher. This will allow users to experience the shared contextual context. This can eventually lead up the ladder if we allow our shared kindred spirit to surface.

Noetic Science

Noetic Science allows for states of insight into depths of truth unplumbed by the discursive intellect. They are illuminations, revelations, full of significance and importance, all inarticulate though they remain; and as a rule they carry with them a curious sense of authority. Very much like becoming a mystic. Noetic sciences was co-founded by Edgar D. Mitchell, an Apollo astronaut who said:

"The simple truth of the universe is that we create our own reality."

If we all commit to sharing meaningful context and begin imagining Utopia as our goal, there will be no stopping the climb up the enlightenment ladder. It will become the reality that Edgar Mitchell refers to.

Because of voice recognition, the knowledge base(s) that Cogitator accesses can be made available to the entire population in whatever language it uses. The world will be connected in truth and understanding.

The follow-up to John Lennon's song tells what we need to achieve peace and well-being on Mother Earth:

"All You Need Is Love"

Love, love, love

Love, love, love

Love, love, love

There's nothing you can do that can't be done

Nothing you can sing that can't be sung

Nothing you can say but you can learn how to play the game

It's easy

Nothing you can make that can't be made

No one you can save that can't be saved

Nothing you can do but you can learn how to be you in time

It's easy

All you need is love

All you need is love

All you need is love, love

Love is all you need

Love, love, love

Love, love, love

Love, love, love

All you need is love

All you need is love

All you need is love, love

Love is all you need

Nothing you can know that isn't known

Nothing you can see that isn't shown

Nowhere you can be that isn't where you're meant to be

It's easy

All you need is love

All you need is love

All you need is love, love

Love is all you need

All you need is love (All together, now!)

All you need is love (Everybody!)

All you need is love, love

Love is all you need

Love is all you need (Love is all you need)

Love is all you need (Love is all you need)

Love is all you need (Love is all you need)

Love is all you need (Love is all you need)

Love is all you need (Love is all you need)

Love is all you need (Love is all you need)

Love is all you need (Love is all you need)

Love is all you need (Love is all you need)

Love is all you need (Love is all you need)

Love is all you need (Love is all you need)

Love is all you need (Love is all you need)

Yee-hai! (Love is all you need)

Love is all you need (Love is all you need)

Yesterday (Love is all you need)

Love is all you need (Love is all you need)

Love is all you need (Love is all you need)

Love is all you need (Love is all you need)

Oh yeah! (Love is all you need)

She loves you, yeah yeah yeah (Love is all you need)

She loves you, yeah yeah yeah (Love is all you need)

Animal trainers used to employ intimidation techniques to make the animals perform unnatural tricks. Many trainers were injured or mauled by their subjects. When love, kindness and compassion is used, not only do the animals perform more happily and willingly, but everyone involved in the spectacle comes away with a feeling of well-being. There is no intimidation allowed in Utopia.

Utopian Handbook

"The fundamental rights of [humanity] are, first: the right of habitation; second, the right to move freely; third, the right to the soil and subsoil, and to the use of it; fourth, the right of freedom of labor and of exchange; fifth, the right to justice; sixth, the right to live within a natural national organization; and seventh, the right to education." Albert Schweitzer

If you want to become a citizen of Utopia, you should familiarize yourself with its composition and objectives. Utopian characteristics are numerous and include:

Peace of Mind

Nothing is more important for a feeling of well-being than having a peaceful mind, free of imaginary concerns and external influences. The day is lived according to four responsibilities:

Taking care of yourself

Taking care of your family and neighbors

Taking care of the community requirements

Taking care of the planet

Wisdom

To become wise, both sides of the brain must be utilized. Wisdom is the understanding created by our innate intelligence accurately interpreting human experience. It is exercised by centering our mind in the Corpus Callosum and using both scientific and artistic capabilities in evaluating experience.

Freedom

No one should be restricted in expressing themselves as long as it does not negatively impact peace.

Responsibility

Utopians accept the fact that they create their own reality.

Participation and contribution

No one is forced or coerced to do anything. Natural Law will shine through.

Education

Children are taught How to learn, not what to learn. They are usually born with much more creativity than adults.

Evolution

The primary objective of Utopians is to grow their understanding. Evolution follows.

Communication

Total honesty and commitment to truth are paramount.

All Utopians live in communities that provide food, shelter and clothing and perform functions related to the purpose of individual communities in concert with all other communities. The knowledge base(s) used to maintain balance in each community will be available to all inhabitants. Nearby communities' knowledge bases will be connected with Local Area Networks (LAN) and the world's knowledge bases will be accessible through Wide Area Networks (WAN.) Every citizen of Utopia is able to communicate with all knowledge bases in whatever language they choose.

Food is supplied by local farming, aquaponics, hydroponics and occasional hunting of wild game. Excess organic material is processed by anaerobic digesters to add to the fresh water and energy supplies. Solids can be used as fertilizer or fuel.

New housing is modular and architecturally pleasing. One important spec detail for builders is blending structures aesthetically with the countryside. Architects create visual art, not just buildings.

There are no clocks or calendars in Utopia. Functions needed to keep the planet and its inhabitants in balance with Natural Law are communicated as they occur.

Do us dreamers a favor and pass this book to others...

The Utopian Community Brain

Community Management

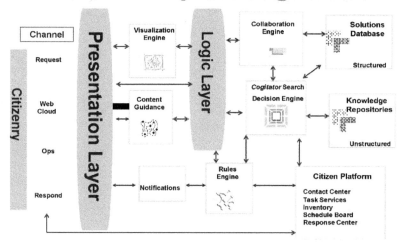

www.ingramcontent.com/pod-product-compliance
Lightning Source LLC
LaVergne TN
LVHW022316060326
832902LV00020B/3494